So You'd Like to Own a Horse?

Pamela Rigby

Published
by
HAPPY HORSE PRESS
Oak House
Newton Hall Lane
Mobberley
Cheshire WA16 7LQ

Tel 01565 889054

www.happyhorsepress.co.uk

© Pamela Rigby 2008
ISBN 978-0-9558286-0-7

Cover design, layout and typesetting
Christine Pemberton

Foreword

I started a small riding school in 1972, with 16 stables and two fields. Most of the riding was hacking out, even the pouring rain didn't prevent riders turning up for their regular slot! Over the years the school gradually expanded and present facilities include 30 stables, two indoor arenas and two outdoor arenas. It is Approved by both the Association of British Riding Schools and the British Horse Society.

During the course of my chosen career I have acquired a wealth of experience, particularly with riders progressing from novices to becoming capable horse owners. Many times I have helped people choose a horse, and am very aware of potential problem areas, as well as the great joy and fulfilment that horse owning can bring.

This book is designed to give guidance on the pathway to owning a horse, which is an extremely personal decision. Over the years, clients had often suggested that I write a book on this subject. Recently I have had the time to put pen to paper and have enjoyed compiling this book, with plenty of reminiscing along the way! Please note that throughout the text all the horses are referred to as 'he', and both horses and ponies are referred to as 'horses'.

In addition to my experience my qualifications include the BHSII and BHS Stable Manager. The Association of British Riding Schools recently awarded me the Fellowship of the Association, of which I am very proud!

I hope that the horse you decide to own is happy being owned by you!

****

.....an invaluable guide for all potential horse owners. A delight to read .....

Dorothy Johnson F.B.H.S.

In praise of the horse

Where in this world can man find nobility without pride, friendship without envy or beauty without vanity?

Here, where grace is laced with muscle, and strength by gentleness confined.

He serves without servility; he has fought without enmity. There is nothing so powerful, nothing less violent; there is nothing so quick, nothing more patient.

England's past has been borne on his back. All our history is his industry; we are his heirs, he our inheritance.

Ladies and gentlemen, ... THE HORSE

courtesy of Ronald Duncan

CONTENTS

Albert Booth - 'The Boss'
1902 - 1988

1
In the Beginning

"Best decision I ever made." - Jean Branson, Redditch
"An addition to the family." - Sandra Harding, Mother of three teenagers
"Horse, dog, cat, me." - Peter, long suffering husband
"The sole cause of our divorce." - Anon - London
"Our family without a pony? No way." - The Roberts family, Chester

It usually begins with the seed of a thought, following an enjoyable ride or time spent with a horse. *"If this were my own horse, I would have this pleasure every day."*

If these thoughts are there, I hope the following chapters will help to give you a practical insight into the issues involved before you allow your thoughts to change from if to when. As a teenager I helped at a small riding school, escorting rides among all the other tasks. The horses that we used as escorts varied wildly (literally at times) as the boss's maxim was *"a good rider can ride any horse at all"* Any comments about not being able to stop, or even go, were met with derision. Of course I developed an attachment to some of the horses, but as I didn't own them, if a buyer came along they went. After a particularly nice horse had been sold, "if" entered my mind.

The event that made me change from 'if' to 'when' was at a show. Whilst I was riding my favourite horse, some people admired him, bought him and took him home in their horsebox. I came home in floods of tears, vowing to have my own horse that could not be sold. This incident, though, did give me another view of horses' behaviour; the buyer of the horse assured me that I was welcome to go and visit him at his new home. Whilst in the field he used to come trotting up when I called his name, which is one of the reasons I liked him so much. When I did go along about three weeks later he was in the field and I immediately called his name. No response! Barbara then whistled, and he trotted over to her! At the time I was upset that he had changed attachment so soon, but realised that in the right home most horses can adapt to differences in ownership without too much stress.

I used to attend horse auctions with the boss if I could get the time off school, so when I started work I began saving for my own horse, still going to the auctions when I could. Quite a few horses appeared ok, but on closer investigation were not ideal. As the stable owner knew all the dealers, he would find out about most of the horses, very necessary at a sale.

Then one day at an auction I saw the perfect looking horse, a palomino, four years old. He appeared very sound and healthy, and according to the man selling him was being sold because his daughter wanted a car. According to the person holding him, he was a bit of a handful, which is why they were not riding him at the sale, but good in traffic. After some nerve racking bidding, he was mine, and when we got home found out why he had been held all the time – he hated being tied up. He was very spirited and I loved him from the moment I sat on him. I had him for 22 years, and he was put down when his quality of life was beginning to deteriorate.

Having factual knowledge will make the horse owning decision easier, so if you acquire a horse you know that the chances of years of enjoyment are far greater than if you wait to deal with situations as they arise. Horses prefer stress free owners!

I have helped many people learn to ride and then progress to becoming owners, and so know many of the situations that need discussion before a horse joins the family, as most horses do become just that! It was great fun researching this aspect of horses and all the owners and riders I spoke to enjoyed recalling their first steps to horse owning, although some had struggled at first as their knowledge was not enough to avoid the pitfalls that can arise. All have given permission for their comments or experiences to be used.

Having a horse in the family can be beneficial to all members. Two parents I know are sure that having a horse gave their teenage children a healthy lifestyle, as most spare time was spent with the horse. The horse becomes a topic of conversation, as one father commented, *"whilst my daughter was between 15 and 17 it was only having to talk about the horse that kept us in communication. Now we laugh about it, but at the time it was so important."*

Often everybody will go to an event; riders and non-riders can be involved and make it a family day out.

The main areas to seriously consider are the costs of care, equipment, veterinary, insurance, competitions and on going training, plus an enormous commitment in time.

Your ability will be a main factor; decide if you want to progress in any sphere, or are you happy to own a horse and carry on riding as you are at present. You may already be a very experienced rider and now want your own horse, or perhaps a relative newcomer to horses. The same situations and considerations need taking into account, regardless of your experience.

There is no age limit to having your first horse. The aptly named 'Silver' was bought for Norice as her Silver Wedding anniversary gift, even though at the time he was unbroken and she was just about mastering rising trot! *"Pam did say at the time it was not an ideal start"*, says Norice, *"but we sent him to her to be broken in and kept on with our lessons. It took about a year before Silver and I developed an understanding, then he was brilliant. He became part of the family and we had him till the end."*

Anne bought her first horse when she was 53, as her children were then experienced enough to share him, although he is 16.2hh. Now, all except Dad are involved in his care, whilst Dad looks after himself over the weekend!

It has been known for grand parents to buy a yearling as a christening present, so as the child grows up the pony will be ready to ride.

Whatever your reasons for owning your own horse, it will bring you endless pleasure for many years and you will never be bored!

2
Costs of Basic Care

"You need to start off with a large fortune, because owning ponies takes a small fortune from you" - Alan, father of two competitive children from Cheshire.
"Worth every penny" - Janet, owner of an old pony and a horse, juggles three part time jobs to pay for her horses.
"The money spent on buying must be considered the tip of the iceberg" - an ex owner who had to sell after 18 months. He had not budgeted for all the expenses on top of basic DIY livery. I quite admire this man, as he did not struggle on to the point where his horse was being affected by lack of funds.

One note of caution: if the proposed purchase is a pony for a child, carry out the costings in secret, so that if the costs are prohibitive the child will never know what may have been!

LIVERY

A place for your horse to live. Usually somewhere that other owners keep their horses. This needs to be a place where you feel that your horse is as safe as possible, even if you are not around, so you need to have faith in the person in charge. A small yard will have a relatively personal feel, whereas a large yard will have more bustle and activity all the time. It is a personal decision to decide which would suit you best.

The reputation and personality of the yard owner is always an important factor as well. This is, after all, the person who will be providing the environment in which you will be spending a considerable amount of your time from now on. Find out the secretary of a local affiliated riding club, who will know many of the stables, good or bad. Local feed merchants and horse shops are also a good place

to ask, and they often have an adverts board. Perhaps the best source of all will be the local farrier!

Unless you know a person already there and happy, phone up some yards in your area and arrange a visit. The owner or manager should be pleased to show you the facilities and discuss the terms with you. The yard should be reasonably clean and orderly even if the buildings are old, and the place should show due regard for health and safety. There should be no old machinery or piles of rubbish lying around.

Look at the stables, they need to be big enough for your horse/pony and have secure bolts at the top and bottom of the door. See what kind of bedding is normally used, even rubber matting needs a cover of absorbent bedding, to prevent the horse becoming smelly. Ask if the electrical wiring is regularly checked and whether there is an electricity supply to the stable. Are there facilities to wash off your horse if it is very muddy, or hot?

Which type of watering system is used? Automatic troughs are very good but it is essential that they are checked daily and are not blocked. Lack of water is very serious.

Talk to some of the clients, as it is important to be at ease with other owners.

It is nice to have company in whatever you do with your horse .....

Some of these people may well become friends later on. Enquire if any of the other owners compete or hack out, as it is nice to have company in whatever you do with your horse. Are there families around or is it mostly adults? Children are usually happier in a place where there are other children to ride with and befriend. Many will loose interest if on their own most of the time, but with friends around the pony becomes part of their lifestyle and a topic of conversation.

If you do not know the yard, it would be an idea to pop in at some time, just to confirm that what had been said does actually happen. I knew a livery yard that mainly had horses belonging to owners who rode at weekends, and they regularly only brushed the parts that showed from under the rugs (legs, and neck), and then exercised them briefly on a Friday. - Full livery. Smart looking place, but lousy stable management. Fortunately, this is an exception to the norm; most people involved in horses are nice people anyway (and usually own a dog, so check the ruling on taking your own dog onto the yard).

The majority of stables are run as commercial businesses by knowledgeable people, so this ensures that clients are well looked after. Large yards become a community, where everyone knows and looks after each other.

I know three couples that met through their horses and are now married!

...... with many lasting friendships formed

Inspect the grazing land, it needs to be sufficiently weed free and not be bare. Lots of droppings and weeds indicates a lack of good pasture management, causing horse-sick field.

It goes without saying that the fencing must be in good repair.

A good fence would be post and rails in front of a hedge
Stone walls are a good shelter, as is a thick hedge.

Left: It would be dangerous to have barbed wire or sheep wire dividing fences, as horses will play or fight over a fence, and serious injuries have been caused by this type of dividing fence.

Below: Note what type of water provision is used, and ask who checks it daily.

If your horse is going to be out in the winter months, the field needs to have some sort of shelter or wind break that provides protection from the wind and driving rain, even if it is just a thick hedge to stand by. A field shelter is used more often in the summer to get away from flies, but can be useful to keep hay dry. These need to be big enough to prevent one horse trapping another in a corner, so do need to be open fronted.

Do the mares and geldings have separate fields or are they all in together? When mares are in season, approximately every three weeks in the summer, geldings may fight over them and be unsettled.

What number of horses live together, small groups or as a herd? There is no hard and fast rule on this as long as there is sufficient grazing to keep the horse healthy, but you need to know these facts before you decide where to go.

Check that the yard owner has care and custody insurance in place for both their clients and horses, in case of an accident arising from their negligence (a rare occurrence, but you need to know).

You should be aware of the opening times of the yard, as it has to fit in with your time as well, especially if you work. Early morning or late evening may be your best times to be with your horse, so this has to be normal open time for the yard, so just another point to check. Opening times vary from place to place.

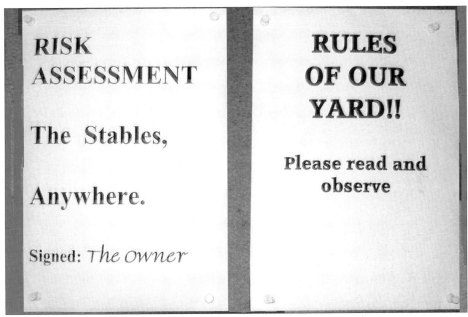

There should be a Risk Assessment in place, available for visitors to read, and a prominent notice to stipulate emergency procedures and contact phone numbers.

All livery yards should ask you to fill in a contract, stating what is included in the costs involved, and just as important, make sure you are aware of anything that is not included. The contract will need your address, contact number, horses details and your vet's number in case they need to get him if you are not there.

There is no law at present to licence livery-only yards and the standards can vary enormously. Do visit a few yards before you decide where to keep your horse. The British Horse Society run an Approval System for livery yards as well as riding schools, but this is purely voluntary.

The best are probably the places that people stay at for years. Don't forget to take the cost of travelling each day into consideration. Are you happy to travel to find the place you want or would you like to be closer to home so that you could

pop out to see the horse more often? The important thing is to know that the horse is in safe hands when you are not around.

Wearing a riding hat to the current BSI Kite mark standard at all times will be a stipulation on livery yards, as their insurance will state that reasonable steps must be taken to keep people safe whilst on their premises. Riders not wearing protective headgear could be construed as the owner of the premises not providing a duty of care. There is no legislation to make it a law that hats should be worn, except for children under 14 on a public highway. Ninety nine percent of riders do this automatically, but the few who do not need to be aware of this ruling.

Different types of livery

DIY means that you care for the horse yourself, with stable and grazing being provided. You do all the work.

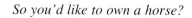

This can mean visiting him twice a day, a large commitment, especially if you go to work, getting up early to check him, mucking out or riding, back home, a change of clothes and going to work/school. In the evening similar routine, change of clothes and out again to the horse. Quite a lot of this may have to be done in the dark, especially in the winter. DIY is great if you enjoy the caring as much as the riding and have the time to enjoy your horse.

There is great satisfaction in creating a good environment for your horse, and having a contented healthy horse, knowing it is all your own work. Many friendships strike up, often sharing some of the daily tasks and holiday cover. When the farrier comes to the horse, he will need him to

be already dry, and under cover if it is raining or very windy. With DIY it will be your responsibility to be there, or arrange for another person to hold the horse. Some yards will charge for this, but usually on DIY there is an exchange system for farrier visits with one person supervising their friends' horses as well as their own.

Points to clarify

Will there be an experienced person over the age of sixteen on site all the time? Experienced help at hand is good even if you are very experienced yourself, as situations such as a horse being cast (where it has rolled close to the wall and become jammed and can't get up) will nearly always needs two people's strength and knowledge to sort out.

Most DIY yards appear to fall into two separate categories. Firstly the stables and grazing are charged for and the owners left to their own devices, which is fine if they are all safety conscious and knowledgeable. But I do know that arguments can occur about such things as which horses go in which field, when to rest a field, who checks water daily or who will remove ragwort or any other poisonous plant if it grows. Who keeps the yard tidy, turns off the lights, locks up etc, can become a bone of contention!

The second category of yard also charges for the stable and grazing, but does have basic rules to be observed which help the yard run without friction. The owner or manager will plan which fields are available, observe accepted land management practises and generally care for the day to day organisation and maintenance.

What is the area of grazing available?

It is much more economical to have lots of grazing, as grass is an excellent feed for the horse and very little extra feed would be needed in summer if the horse is not in hard work. The downside is that the horse may not want to be caught if there is plenty of food around!

Too much grass can cause a horse to become overweight, so it is your responsibility to keep a check on this. Obesity in horses can cause joint problems, as well as the well known and serious laminitis (not the only cause of laminitis, but a main one).

If the grazing is insufficient extra food (hay) will be essential and must be provided in with the livery charge.

What, if any, is the amount of supervision provided for children to be at the yard on their own?

I have witnessed a lovely little lad, quietly playing with a box of matches, collecting handfuls of hay and straw and chortling away at the sight of the little bonfires he was making, underneath the hay store! On the darker side, two older children were threatening a younger child regularly, and it was only when I

suspected there was a problem that this came to light. Needless to say the policy on unsupervised children changed overnight! Nearly all places assume that the parents will be the supervisor at all times so this needs taking into account. Many DIY yards have a lower age limit for children. Some are adults only!

Normal Health & Safety precautions should be in place and followed. Some of the rules may seem over the top, but they are there for your protection and you have a duty of care to follow the instructions. The yard owner is responsible for providing a safe place and you are responsible for your actions. Gone are the days when nobody wore hats, and ponies were ridden about in headcollars, bareback.

Do I need my own tools for mucking out?

Some places provide the equipment; this is fine if people need to use it at differing times, but you may need your own, clearly named! Find out the procedure about the muck heap, as usually you have to throw your muck high onto the heap daily to prevent it from spreading all over the yard. Some yards have a tractor and driver who do this on a regular basis.

Is there a place for my rugs etc?

Wet New Zealand rugs take up a lot of room when they need hanging up to dry, which can take days. Make sure they are named, as dirty rugs can look similar. If there is not this facility available, you will need to set aside an area at home, and rugs can be smelly! A rug rack for general use would be a bonus.

Is there a secure place for my feed, hay, straw and tools?

Unfortunately, there are some dishonest people who also own horses, and it has been known for hay and food and even rugs to go missing on DIY yards. I know of a case where the culprit used to go round all the other boxes and take some hay from each horse for his own. Every night. He probably took a bit from all the feed bins as well. The best solution is for each owner to have an area which can be locked, so that temptation is removed.

Is there electricity all the time?

The stable needs to have a light, but electricity meters are installed in some places on arenas so you will need a supply of whichever coins are needed, to avoid being plunged into darkness. If the supply is metered, always have a torch at hand, so you can find your way to the car to put the headlights on or get more money.

Is there an arena or good hacking?

An arena is not essential, although is convenient if you prefer to school your horse, or lunge him (if lungeing is allowed in the arena as it can damage the membrane). Some riders never go out on the road, some combine both, others prefer to ride out all the time it is a personal choice. Get an Ordnance Survey map of the area to give you an idea of the off road riding.

Drive around the local roads to assess the level of traffic on the roads or lanes at the times you will normally ride. There may be a hazard such as a pig farm, (horses

often do not like the smell) that is not very obvious at first. Roads that are very busy in the mornings can be quiet during the day, ideal if you ride at that time. Take into account that during the winter your riding time is limited by daylight.

Is there a charge for the arena and can it be booked?

This is an important point to clarify, whether your livery be full or DIY, as a communal arena can be great if all goes well, but can cause ill feeling if a horse is being a problem either to its owner or by upsetting the others. If you needed to practise a dressage test or put up a course of jumps, you would need the whole arena. Livery at a riding school or competition yard could mean it is not available at all times. Sometimes the livery charge will include use of the arena, or it may be an extra charge.

Can the horse be turned out all year round?

Some stables have a policy of not turning horses out during winter months, mainly because of the damage that is caused to the land when it is wet. The fields will become very muddy and the following year the grazing will be less. Farmers have told me that horses run around much more than cows and so damage the fields.

To my mind, regular turn out is essential, even in a limited space, as unless you can ride every day it is not fair to have the horse stabled all the time, especially during the winter, rugged up. Daily exercise is needed to work off energy, and keep the horse's metabolism working, so an hour's walk is not sufficient for most stabled horses. He will have excess energy to get rid of and to ride an exuberant horse could be more than you bargained for.

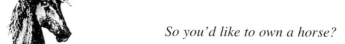

I have bought numerous horses and ponies that were being sold because the owners had become scared of them for a variety of reasons. The main reason was that the horse had changed character, usually for the worst. Friendly ones can start biting, horses normally good in traffic begin shying, well-behaved ones buck for no reason that you can see, and most had become jumpy. The common factor with these horses was that they were stabled all the time. With sufficient work and appropriate feed, together with time in the field, they were happier and reverted back to their true personality.

Apart from the safety angle, horses need to socialise with each other, as they are herd animals and they often groom each other on the neck or graze together. If they are in the field regularly they are less likely to gallop round just for the feeling of freedom!

If you compete, are there facilities for your discipline on site or nearby for you to use/hire?

It is best to check if there is transport available to hire , unless you have your own. If so, could it be parked up at the stables and would there be a charge?

Are there set times for feeding etc?

Horses are more settled if they are in a routine, so find out the feeding regime at the yard. Quite often owners club together to share morning or evening feed times, which is better for the horses. It can be distracting if you are grooming but your horse can hear next door being fed and starts fidgeting, or you lead your horse past another that is being fed outside it's box. All it takes is one of them to kick out and you have an injured horse. Keeping to a regular feeding routine is one of the ways of keeping a stress free horse!

If I am ill or on holiday is there provision for someone to look after my horse?

Most owners have friends who can provide holiday cover, but you may want to go on holiday with that friend! Yard owners will always help out in a crisis, but you need to be organised for illness/holiday cover.

Cost of monthly food, hay, bedding

It is fairly common practise for the yard owner to provide hay and straw/shavings for owners to buy, it will then go on the bill. You will not have to store these bulky items as they are bought when needed. Otherwise have a dry vermin proof place as a store at your home. Try to calculate how much your horse will use, as together

with the hard feed these are considerable costs, which may narrow the choice between DIY and full livery.

GRASS LIVERY

Horses with a respiratory problem can be kept healthy by living out all year round. Living outside is a horse's natural lifestyle, but in the wild state there would be a very large area to roam, with very few boundaries. On grass livery you pay a rent for the grazing only and may or may not have the use of a stable. Your horse lives out all year round and you fit your riding and horse care according to the seasons. The horse is living its life as nature intended, constantly grazing and taking small amounts of water. Feed costs will depend on the quality of the grazing, and the amount of work your horse is expected to do. It could be approximately the same for any concentrate feed, maybe more in the winter, as supplementary hay would be needed. It can be a less expensive way to keep your horse if you are experienced enough to realise when the horse can be worked hard and when not.

The quality of the grazing would be an important factor in deciding to use this system. The horse would nearly always be kept in a herd situation, keeping as close to nature as possible.

If the horse is working normally and clipped, a New Zealand rug would be used, but you would need at least two in case one was ripped. As long as you had the horse's feet regularly trimmed and not shod, this could be the most economical way to keep your horse.

FULL LIVERY

This usually entails everyday care of the horse, providing all mucking out, bedding, hay, feed, turning out and fetching in from the field. Some interpretations of full

will not include grooming or tacking up ready to ride, but most owners wish to do this themselves anyway. It would be one of the items to be clarified on your contract before you started at the stables. Grooming is a very satisfactory part of horse owning, and bonds the relationship with the horse, and you can take pride in having a smart, gleaming horse. Make sure that you have an input into the amount of food he receives, so that you can alter his diet if you feel it is necessary depending on his condition and behaviour

Normal Health & Safety precautions should be in place and followed, and you will have a contract stating what is included in the charge.

Points to clarify

Is there an experienced person on site at all times?
Establish who is in charge of supervising the care of your horse, especially checking daily water supply, mucking out and turning out. Get clarification that only people covered on the yard's insurance care for your horse! This is an important factor, as you may not see your horse every day, as you would at DIY. Usually you give written permission for the stable owner to call a vet if needed.

Who will actually carry out the mucking out, changing rugs, catching, etc? Accidents can happen at the best of places but to minimise these there must be an experienced person in charge of your horse. Some yards have students or helpers experienced in stable duties though they may still need supervision.

Beware of enthusiastic children being allowed to care for your horse, as one small mistake in handling a situation can turn into an accident!

What type of hard and bulk food is normally used?

Find out how much and what type of feed is given each day and be prepared to be involved in changing the quantities if it is deemed necessary. There is a mantra - 'feed according to the work expected'. The horse can be getting fitter and not doing sufficient work, so would need the hard feed stopping or reducing drastically and replacing by bulk. Or he may be being asked to work hard without sufficient feed and so losing weight. A caring yard owner will suggest if the feed needs changing.

Are lessons available if you want them?

Once they own a horse, many riders keep on with regular lessons and training. You will get used to people saying *'why do you still have lessons, can't you do it yet?'*

It is the same adage as in any other sport; you never stop progressing. Learning new skills gives a buzz, although to a non-rider, hearing about your perfect working trot/ shoulder in is a foreign language. How often do you hear *'all you appear to do is go round in circles'*? My answer is *'golfers just hit a ball then follow it and swimmers simply swim up and down'.* (only kidding!)

Is there an arena, can you book it for your use and is there a charge?

As in DIY, sometimes it is good to have an empty arena to ride in, especially if you are schooling and need to concentrate. The type of yard you are on will have an effect on the availability of the facilities. If the place hires out the arena to outsiders, it may not always be available when you want it. The use of an arena is sometimes part of the livery package.

What is the hacking like in the area?

As in the section about DIY

Can the horse be turned out regularly?

As in the section for DIY

Can tack be left and would your insurance cover still be provided?

Do check the cover carefully, as often the insurance is not valid if there is no sign of forced entry. I know of a case where tack had been stolen during the day, whilst the tack room had been left open as people were still about working on the yard. As there was no sign of forced entry the insurance was void. Another set of tack was not insured as it was amongst tack stolen from a riding school, but the insurance only covered it at the owner's home.

What security is in place?

In most places the security will be fine, as owners will look after their property and possessions. Just check to ensure that any property you leave will be safe. Horse trailers seem to be a target for thieves, and have been taken in broad daylight where no one has questioned them about hitching up and driving away. On a large busy yard not all clients will know the friends or acquaintances of all other owners and therefore strangers may not be noticed. A trailer belonging to a Disabled Riders group was stolen from my yard after being taken to a show. The thieves must have followed it back, watched the people unhitch, lock up and go. They then broke the gate lock and trailer lock and it was gone without trace.

Is there a different charge during summer months?

Occasionally charges vary if the horse lives out all summer and does not use a stable.

If the livery is at a busy riding school or competition yard, bear in mind that the facilities will often be in use at prime riding times.

WORKING LIVERY

This is usually at a riding school or college, where the stables work the horse as part payment towards the livery price. It can work well if you have a limited time available.

Points to clarify

How many hours will the horse work and when?

This will depend on the level of the horse's fitness when the agreement starts and how often you plan to ride yourself. Arrange in advance the times and conditions, to suit both parties, and you should end up with a fit, well-behaved horse. Regular progressive work is so important to keep your horse sound in mind as well as body.

Will most riders be of a similar standard to you?

This is the area that causes most problems with working livery, as the owners will not always agree about the people riding their horse. I have known it be that they do not like the person, regardless of their ability. Working livery demands a degree of trust between both parties, with the horse's welfare at the heart of the issue.

Will the horse need extra insurance in a riding school?

They usually do. Do remember to inform the insurance company if situations change, as a riding school horse insurance is usually dearer.

Who pays for the shoeing, worming, etc?

Normally the owner's responsibility, but it should be mentioned in the contract.

Who is responsible for tack cleaning, grooming, etc?

There is no hard and fast rule on these tasks, they need to be arranged at the start of each contract.

This system works well if a structured agreement is made in advance and the horse is kept to the same level of training.

PART LIVERY

This system can be interpreted in many ways, but all the above points are relevant. Friends of mine run a system that works well where the horse is cared for during the week, and then the owner cares for him at the weekend.

Another popular system is having a list of services available, priced separately, so you choose which services you need to pay for, and which you will do yourself. These flexible systems can work very well if you have a varied degree of spare time.

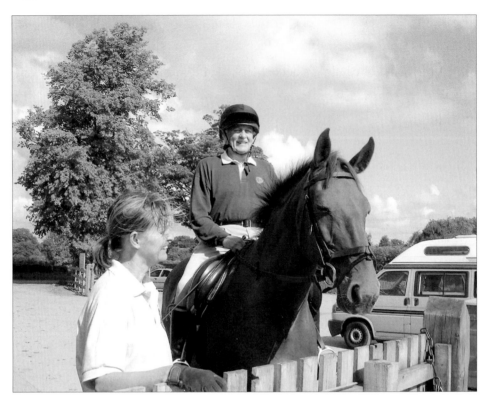

SHARED OWNERSHIP

This option is increasing in popularity, providing two owners with differing spare times or preferences to enjoy the benefits of having a horse. The costs and work are shared, and provide an ideal solution to owners with varying commitments. I know of one partner caring for the horse each morning and during the daytime whilst her children are at school and the other partner is at work, and then partner two takes over responsibility in the evenings and weekends. Both riders and the horse are happy and two people can afford the time and money. There can be many variations on this theme and provided there is a binding agreement between the partners of procedures in case of illness/accident to the horse, this can be a successful arrangement.

A tiny word of caution; a horse I looked after, which belonged to two people, became the subject of a legal battle, as the owners fell out and both failed to pay the bills. Tricky… This is why the agreement needs drawing up in advance.

One important question to ask yourself about all livery options –
How would I feel about paying for livery if the horse was off work? The financial outgoing would be the same, or even more if the horse was on box rest, but obviously the horse could not be ridden.

For example, a sprained tendon can require complete box rest for a few weeks, then only walking for a month. A torn ligament can take six months to heal and then another three months to get back to fitness. This horse will probably become the best groomed horse on the yard! You will be paying out and not riding.

Paying for livery if the horse is ill

This is a point that deters quite a few potential owners. Some horses carry on through life with no injuries, whilst others are accident-prone. The fact that you are a perfect owner will not prevent accidents or problems, so be prepared for some character building incidents!

OWN LAND

Probably the most economical way to keep a horse, provided you are confident in providing year round care for the horse and know all the signs of good and bad health. You will need to be able to recognise and deal with all poisonous plants, as on a livery yard you presume that the owner checks for this! (See section under Welfare)

One of the people I questioned before writing this section told me it had not proved to be economical yet, as he had recently moved his horses onto his six acre field and had to buy a small tractor, harrows, pasture topper and a barn to keep them in! Before the horses came the field was cared for by a farmer, who looked after the field in return for the hay crop. When there were horses on the field, no hay could be made, so the arrangement dissolved.

Points to clarify
Availability of stable or field shelter

Even if the horse lives out all year round, a stable or shelter will be useful for tacking up and grooming, under cover, maybe for feeding in bad weather. Hopefully the horse will never be ill or injured, but a stable would be needed instantly in these situations. One good system is to have access to the stable from the field, so the horse can go in and out as he pleases.

Is the grazing adequate and well fenced?

The quality of the grazing is more important than the acreage, it will need to be managed to provide year round turn out. One area only may be used in winter to avoid all the land being damaged.

So you'd like to own a horse?

On a small area set aside time to collect the droppings regularly, or arrange harrowing for large areas. There will need to be more than one paddock so they can be used in rotation, one being grazed whilst the other being rested or fertilised weed controlled. Horses on small areas may need extra food at times.

Ragwort is difficult to eradicate, so if it is around it will need digging up and burning straight away. It is poisonous if eaten and although horses do not normally eat it whilst it is growing, wilted or dried plants are palatable. Eating small amounts over a time can be serious, even fatal.

Are water & electricity on site?

Not absolutely essential, but life will be much harder without these basics. Carrying water to a field can be back breaking, and being in a stable in the dark, without lighting, is not ideal.

Will I feel happy riding on my own most of the time or could I have another person as company, with their horse?

This is a personal decision, as another person could be intrusive on your property, but having a companion could outweigh this. It is often very relaxing to have company whilst hacking out.

Have I the time to attend to the horse every day?

The biggest decision of all is every day care. If you have the time and knowledge to enjoy having your horse at home it can be the ultimate choice. Your horse will be in sight all day long, and can be visited whenever you want.

Will my horse be settled living on his own?

This is a hard question to answer as some horses appear to be very settled on their own, which seems to go against the naturally accepted fact that they are herd animals. If there are other animals in close proximity this can help, as can constant attention from a human. I know one horse that lives very contentedly with a llama and another who shares his field with chickens. The down side is that if your horse is not one of these relaxed types, he will be stressed and could damage himself trying to break out and find company.

You would need to know his background before keeping him on his own. Sheep and goats are said to be good company, although I know of one poor goat that was bought to be a companion for a horse that needed box rest. Even though the box was large the horse did not settle, so the goat was duly introduced to the horse, which promptly attacked it!

Is there a place to store the food, bedding and tools?

These will need storing undercover to prevent waste, and steps will need to be taken to make the area as vermin proof as possible.

How much will my monthly food, hay and bedding cost?

These may be able to be bought in bulk which can be economical if none is wasted. You are not paying anyone for the time spent in preparing feeds, filling nets etc, so this is where the savings are made.

Maintenance

You will be responsible for the cost of hedge cutting, harrowing and rolling, drainage, weeding etc.

At some time the horse may need stabling, so if there is not one already, you will have to consider the cost of erecting a stable and the hard standing around it.

Who will look after my horse if I am away?

There will have to be arrangements in place for any time you are away, such as a 'horse sitter' or a place arranged for him to go and stay at these times.

3
EQUIPMENT

"The car is now relegated to the drive as the garage holds all my horse stuff". -
DIY owner Janice, still smiling as her car rusts away

"Our ponies like the latest fashions just like us" – Jessica and Sofia, fashion conscious
eight year olds – lime coloured jodhpurs and cerise hats, with matching numnahs for their
ponies!

"My horse suits pink, so that is the colour of her wardrobe" – Normally sensible
owner when questioned as to why her horse had all pink rugs/boots/headcollars.

Basics

Headcollars x 2.

- Usually made from nylon. The ones with eyelets are best, as they can be fitted
  and will not slip.

- Often get lost or 'borrowed'.

- Leather ones obviously cost a lot more, preferable if you do a lot of travelling,
  as leather is said to break more easily in an emergency.

Stable rugs x 2

- Nowadays made from varying types of materials, with differing "togs" to use
  depending on the time of year and warmth required. One lady still phones the
  local weather forecast each day to see what the night time temperature will
  be, then she decides which rug to put on her horse. At the last count she had
  seven rugs, with varying "togs"

- One will always need to be in the wash, so two is minimum if you rug the
  horse up. Remember, if the horse wears rugs, some of his food will be
  converted to energy as he will not be using it all to create warmth.

- Rugs need washing as often as you decide, every week, or at the end of the winter. Most domestic washing machines won't take a full size rug and it may have to go to be cleaned, another extra cost. Many rugs become ripped and will need repairs.

- You can still buy the original jute rugs, but most people have the nylon ones.

New Zealand/Turnout Rugs 2

- Not essential, as horses are ok out in the rain and cold with thick coats, but are needed for clipped or thin skinned horses, out in the field in winter.

- These can be used for full time wear in the winter, to keep the horse warm and dry all the time, so he can live out night and day. They will need to be checked twice daily, so quite a big decision to use them all the time.

- The rugs made from breathable nylon seem to be the best and dry quicker.

- Rugs should be waterproof, but need constant attention to ensure the proofing stays sound.

- If the rug leaked the poor horse would be cold and wet. (The rug would have pressed the hair flat and close to the skin, and the weight of the rug would press the water onto the skin. Without a rug the hair would have been away from the skin, so the water would run off the hair and not touch the skin, as nature intended). The New Zealand rugs are often used when a horse is turned out for a few hours either to keep him warm, or nearly as important, to keep him clean.

- For competitors, you can have a travelling rug, with your initials on, or a lightweight one just to keep him clean when on a journey.

Other rugs

- There are moisture wicking rugs for use after a horse has been bathed, or is sweating after working. They will need to be changed when the horse has dried off.

  A cotton rug is used in warm weather, especially for travelling.

  Show rugs are often made of wool and have a contrasting binding, with the riders initials on the corner.

Grooming

- The basic kit is essential: Dandy brush with the hard bristles, for use on field kept horses to remove mud and top dirt. It can be used to remove stains on a stabled horse as long as the horse is not clipped or thin skinned.

- The body brush has shorter softer hairs and it is used in conjunction with the curry comb, which is used to comb through the hairs on the body brush, not the horse! The body brush will soon be full of dust and grease, which is why it needs this combing action by the curry comb. The body brush can be used to brush out the mane and tail, unless it is very thick when a comb would work better.

- A water brush has long soft bristles, usually moistened to dampen the mane to help it lie flat and look smarter. It can also be used to wash off the feet if they are muddy.
- Sponges are dampened and used to clean the horses eyes, nostrils and dock area, as well as sponging any stable stains, so you will need a few of these.
- The hoof pick will be in constant use, self explanatory. Hoof oil is applied to make the horse look smarter, but is not essential, as his own natural oils will keep the hoof wall coated.
- The stable rubber is for giving a final finish to the horse's coat, but it is a good idea to lay the other articles out on this, to stop them from being covered in shavings or straw.

The basic kit can rapidly grow as there are dozens of extras on the market.

In addition chalk block is used on white markings, and you can buy shampoos for white horses, or bays or chestnuts. A sweat scraper makes it easier to remove the excess water from the wet hair. After washing the tail, there is a hair de tangler which you can spray on to keep the tail looking nice. To give an appearance of healthy skin Vaseline can be applied to the skin around the eyes and on the muzzle. To pull the mane there is a smaller mane comb, and you will need plaiting thread to be able to plait the mane. Following a thorough grooming, the tail can be moistened and a tail bandage put on and be left for a couple of hours. When it is removed the tail hair will be flat and smart looking.

The strapping pad is for using when you are serious about getting the horse fit. As it is used solely on the main muscles, your anatomy needs to be spot on, and expert help will be useful to demonstrate efficient use.

The pieces that should get most use are the hoofpick, dandy and body brushes along with the curry comb and sponges. Old towels always come in handy, and you obviously need a box to keep all this equipment safe and to hand.

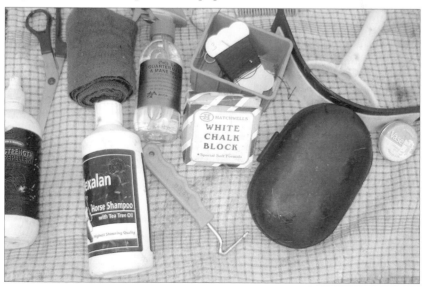

With the fly repellent, experiment to see if you can use an aerosol type on your horse. If it is scared of the noise, buy a liquid form repellent. Horse flies can cause horses to gallop round the field to try and get away from them, and some horses, mine included, are allergic to the bite and break out in lumps all over the body. Quite scary the first time it happened .

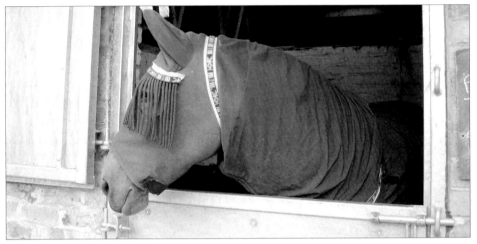

A horse with sweet itch will require a lot of extra effort and fly repellent to keep him comfortable as soon as the midges season starts. He will need constant protection from the midge bites, and possibly keeping in the stable during the day, and fetching in again very early before the midges start up. Protective hoods and rugs can help to alleviate the itching.

First Aid kits

- You will need a thermometer. Horse normal temperature is 100.5 F or 38C, and is taken per rectum, so expert assistance may be needed at first!

- It is a good idea to take your horses temperature when he is well and calm so that you know what is normal as some are naturally lower or higher.

- Scissors to trim any hair from around a wound or cut elastoplast.

- Antibacterial solution such as Hibiscrub, for cleaning wounds
- Animalintex as a poultice
- Gamgee, which is cotton wool covered by gauze, as padding under a bandage
- An elasticated bandage
- Elastoplast or Vetrap, which sticks to itself, very useful for foot bandaging
- Non adherent gauze for dressing wounds
- Cotton wool for cleaning wounds
- A clean container/bucket

Most vets will sell an equine first aid kit, or you can make up your own. Learn to be familiar with the contents, so you can use all the equipment. Being able to take the horses temperature is vital, as a high temperature going un-noticed for 24 hours can change a mild infection into a serious one. Temperature is the first thing to check if a horse has not eaten his feed. Any rise needs professional treatment straight away as it can be the sign of a serious or mild problem. Always take a First Aid kit with you if you travel with the horse, so you may need a second set, and keep one in your transport vehicle.

Saddle, with stirrups and girths

Unless you have the luxury of a very experienced person to help you, this will need fitting by a saddler who will need to see you ride on the saddle to fit it correctly, and check that the saddle spreads the riders weight evenly. Horses vary so much in shape that I could not give details of how to fit a saddle, it is a job for an expert to study each horse. The saddle will need to fit both you and the horse, so fitting can be quite a lengthy business. Saddles need to sit on the muscle at the side of the backbone and avoid touching or pinching the spine. A rider with a long thighbone will need a longer saddle flap. Check to make sure that the top of your boot does not catch on the bottom of the saddle flap. Most saddles are made from leather of differing qualities. Steer clear of very cheap tack as it probably will be inferior quality leather and just as important, inferior stitching, which is dangerous. The important aspect of the saddle is the quality of the tree and workmanship, plus the main task you will need it for.

An ill fitting saddle will cause discomfort or pain to the horse, and place the rider out of balance. Any of these points will cause the horse to change its attitude to being ridden, such as napping, bucking and refusing jumps, although these problems can be rider or joint problem related as well!

A good quality general purpose saddle is the choice of most riders, until they concentrate on one particular discipline. Sizes are measured from the centre of the cantle to the stud at the side of the pommel. Make sure that the buckles and stirrups are stainless steel. Horrible accidents have happened with soft metal stirrups, a horse has fallen and squashed the stirrup iron onto the rider's foot. Luckily, in the case I saw, the stirrup leather came away. The stirrup irons need to be the right size for your foot, again, check with an experienced person when buying them. Cheap buckles or stitching on inferior stirrup leathers can give way under quite mild pressure, with awful results. So, don't skimp on the quality of tack. Synthetic saddles have now become commonplace and are much lighter than conventional leather. Most are on the same styles, although endurance saddles are based on a military style, which spreads the weight over as wide an area as possible, needed on the very long distances they travel.

The correct fit of a saddle is crucial to the horse's comfort

If in doubt do consult a qualified saddler.

Bridle

The quality needs to be the same as the saddle. Sizes are Shetland, Pony, Cob and full size. You can have any colour of browband to suit yourself.

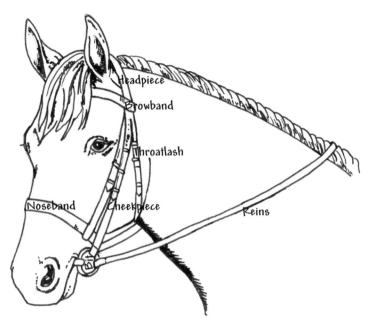

Parts of the Bridle

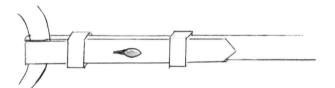

Billet stud fastening, always to the inside.

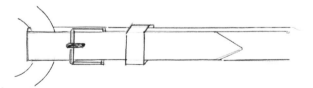

Buckle fastening, always to the outside.

Parts of the bridle

- Head piece, which fits just behind the ears, but not pressing against them.
- The throatlash is narrow and is a part of the headpiece
- Two Cheek pieces, which buckle onto the headpiece at one end and fasten onto the bit at the other, with a buckle or billet fastening.
- Browband, which needs to be the size to hold the headpiece in position.
- Noseband, various sorts, this one is a cavesson noseband.
- Bit- the fit is made by altering the position of the cheekpieces where they buckle onto the headpiece.

Reins

The reins have either buckle fastenings, which fasten on the outside, or billet / stud fastenings which fasten on the inside and are considered neater.

The bit and parts of the bridle will usually be bought separately. Use the same type and size of bit for your new horse that he had before, don't change it straight away.

Parts of a saddle

- The tree is the framework of the saddle that you cannot see. It determines the size and fit of the saddle. If it gets broken the saddle is not safe to use.
- Pommel - The front arch which NEVER EVER should touch the horse's backbone
- Gullet, the channel underneath that holds the saddle clear of the backbone
- Cantle, the back of the saddle
- Seat, self explanatory.
- Skirt - the small piece that covers the stirrup bar
- Stirrup bar. This has a catch at the end that needs to be down whilst you are riding, so in the event of a fall, the Stirrup leather is more likely to come off.
- Stirrup irons need to be the correct size for your foot, and can be conventional

Parts of the Saddle

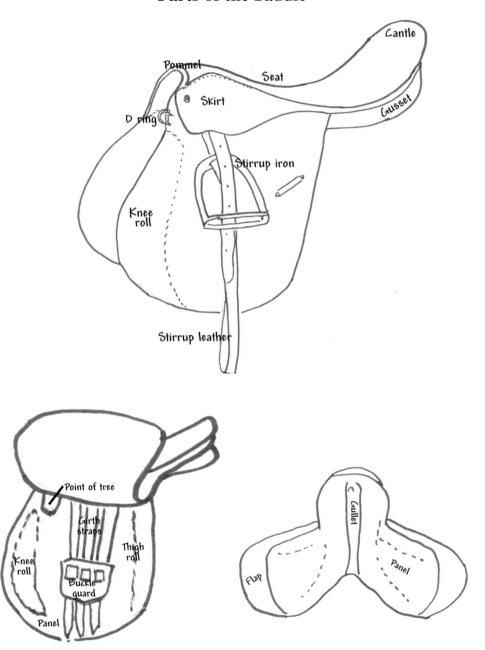

or safety type.

- The saddle flap is the large area that your leg rests on, you lift it to see the
- Girth straps. These are attached to the tree and many of them have a buckle guard so that the buckle does not wear the underneath of the saddle flap.
- Panel is the part next to the horses back, can be the same size as the saddle flap (full panel) or only part way down the saddle flap (half panel)
- Knee roll. The position and thickness of this will influence the type of saddle
- Girth. Many types.

Numnahs or Saddlecloths x 3

A saddle needs to be fitted without a numnah, but most people use one as a slight shock absorber or simply to keep the underneath of the saddle clean. It must always be pulled firmly up in the gullet of the saddle, otherwise it would press on the spine and become a problem. A thick one will make the fit differ, as it will make the horses back be wider, so you would have to be careful if your horse was rotund! On the other hand, if a horse was going to be rounding his back as in jumping high and wide, the thick one would be more comfortable when the horses back was arched.

One will always be in the wash, so usually you will acquire a collection. A numnah is the same shape as the saddle whereas a saddlecloth is a square.

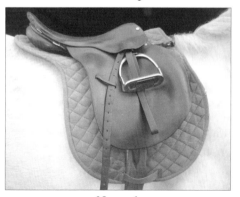

Numnah

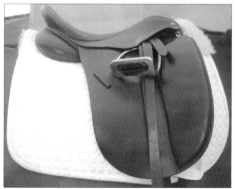

Saddlecloth

So you'd like to own a horse?

Tack cleaning materials

- You will need a selection of sponges and either a bar of saddle soap or a spray soap. A chamois leather is best for drying the leather before soaping, or an old towel. Metal polish and rags for the stirrups and bit rings, but never the mouthpiece - it tastes horrid!

- Buckets, so you don't use the kitchen sink.

- You will need a leather dressing oil to use occasionally to keep the leather supple. Each time tack is cleaned it needs checking for any wear, so it can be mended before an accident can happen. You may even buy two bridles and keep one as best. A cupboard to keep this entire kit safe.

If a saddle needed replacing after a while, due to horse changing shape, or a different rider needed a different size or style of saddle, this cost needs to be taken into consideration.

Extras

- Spare reins, (rubber grip reins are good if you are riding in the rain, or any situation where more grip is needed). Reins are often broken if the horse is left tacked up, but not tied up.

- Different sized stirrup irons if the horse is to be ridden by differing sized riders. A small foot could slide through a large iron, or your foot become jammed in a small iron. Ideally the stirrup iron should have half inch spare each side of your foot. If two different sized riders share the horse, they are best to have their own sized leathers and irons.

- Whips, one short and one longer schooling whip.

- Rugs for drying/travelling.

- If DIY, tools and feed bins and buckets.

- Hay net. You always seem to need an extra one of these.
- Any extra feed you may decide to use, to go faster, slower, slimmer, fatter, more nutritious. Bear in mind that horsey fashions can change, next year's rugs will be better must haves, according to the adverts!

  This equipment list could soar to include a change of car that can pull a trailer!

Boots

Brushing boots are not essential, but are commonly used to protect the horse from knocking one fetlock with the side of the other hoof. This can happen if the horse is turning suddenly, as in jumping, or if any sideways movements are being performed.

- Over reach boots. These go around the pastern and cover the hoof and most importantly the heel area. Used as a precaution to prevent the heel from being injured, especially if the horse is galloping or jumping, when the hind foot comes to the ground before the front foot has moved. Often used when a horse is turned out in the field to prevent him from pulling off a shoe by treading on the heel of a fore foot.
- Travelling boots

  Shaped to fit the hind leg and front leg, these boots protect the legs whilst the horse is travelling. The areas that need most protection are the hocks, knees and pasterns and coronet.

Extra kit for yourself

- Spare jodhs, jeans, boots and gloves.
- If you are going to compete: show jacket, leather boots or leather gaiters and boots, beige jodhpurs, plus baggy trousers to wear over these whilst you sort out your horse at the show.
- Hi viz tabard if you hack out or take your horse across a road

- Spare riding hat
- Spare waterproofs
- Magazine subscription or books
- Membership of the British Horse Society. Whilst joining is not compulsory, it is well worth the annual fee to keep up to date with news and events in British equestrianism.

Two well turned out girls with their horse, Flint, and tack,
just returning from a successful show.
Rugs, bucket and grooming kit have just been unloaded from
their small modern horse box.

4
VETERINARY COSTS AND CONSIDERATIONS

'I would not buy a car without an MOT, so I won't buy a horse without one' -
John, now owning his third horse
'Having a full veterinary insurance policy gave me peace of mind, even though I never had to use it' -
Jennifer, responsible owner
'When our horse had to have an emergency operation for a twisted gut, we were so relieved that we could have him treated without worrying about the cost' -
Pat and Terry, ideal owners

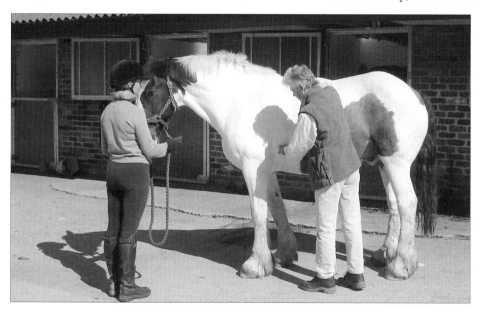

Don't forget the cost of initial vetting before purchase. Choose a vet in your area, with experience of horses, so that this vet can be involved with your horse's ongoing welfare whilst you own it. Better still, register with a vet before you make your purchase. When the vet I used for my horses announced that he was going to retire, I immediately approached another vet who specialised in horses, to see if he would take on the general care of all 40+ horses. This was before any of them needed veterinary attention, as often vets are called out in emergencies, and need to know your location. Having to suddenly find a vet experienced in horses would have been a tall order. Because the same Veterinary Group treats the horses, they are familiar with the history and management of them. This is a very important factor in making a diagnosis and arranging subsequent after care.

One aspect of veterinary care is the vaccination of the horses against flu and tetanus. This is, in my opinion, a cost not to be economised on, even though not compulsory. If you ever saw a horse with tetanus you would appreciate how awful it is, nearly always fatal. The annual cost of vaccinating 40 horses is obviously high, but the fact that over the last 20 years we have never had an outbreak of flu speaks for itself. Each new horse is vaccinated on arrival, with the appropriate boosters at two and six months and then each year they are all lined up, and within an hour all are up to date. The vet keeps a record of when the tetanus plus flu booster injection is needed, and will change the brand if he thinks it beneficial.

Pre Purchase Vetting

A Pre Purchase Examination involves five stages (vetting)

First stage

The vet will examine the horse at rest and look at and feel its limbs and joints. Any lumps and bumps and blemishes will be examined and noted. He will check the horse's back and also note how it stands and behaves. The horse's heart and lungs will be listened to at rest, and the feet checked for being in balance and healthy. The horse's teeth and mouth are inspected, and although it is possible to determine the approximate age of a horse by examining the teeth, the vet cannot legally be

responsible for giving an exact age, as there are so many influences affecting the appearance of the teeth. Any mouth or tooth problems can be serious. The horse's eyes will be examined, preferably in a darker area.

Second stage

Outside, the vet will study the conformation of the horse, as this can have an effect on the long term soundness and ability for the job expected of it. The horse will be led up at walk and trot whilst the vet watches the way the horse moves, and hopefully notes that it is not lame. Often lungeing will take place, on both reins, as a slight lameness would show on circles, even though it did not show on the straight.

Third stage

The horse is then ridden/worked as much as his fitness dictates, to increase his heart and respiration rate. These will be taken when the horse is worked, to check that the difference between rates at rest and work are normal. It will be preferable if it was you who rode the horse, so the vet could note the temperament with you on board, and maybe comment on it.

Fourth stage

The horse's breathing will be listened to as the exercise is taking place and afterwards. After the exercise, the horse will be rested for a while. If all is well, the vet will fill in a certificate noting his findings. It is usually at this stage that the seller is asked to state if the horse is free from any vices, as a vet would not generally be able to tell during the handling of the horse.

Fifth stage

The horse will be trotted up once more after resting, and a heart rate and lung check will be repeated. A blood sample will be taken, which is stored at an official laboratory for six months. However it would be analysed in the case of a horse going lame soon after it changed hands. (The preserved sample would show up any drugs in his system at the time of purchase).

Most vets will want to know what the horse's main job will be, as some minor problems won't affect performance for a leisure horse, but would for a competition career. Vets are good at being aware of horses' temperaments and most will be happy to discuss their thoughts with you.

If the horse is bought during the winter months, ask the owner to confirm that the horse does not have sweet itch. (which is not always obvious in the winter, but it would deter most potential owners as the management of this can be very time consuming)

There may be minor points mentioned on the certificate which would not affect the horse for working, just make sure that the insurance company will accept these if they have asked for a certificate.

The vet will need to see the passport to note the number. Equine passports are now compulsory, and there is a fine for owners not having one for their horse. There will be a diagram showing any white markings, blemishes and whorls (when the hair grows in different directions and forms a swirl). The breeder and subsequent owners need to be on this document, any new owner sends the passport to the initial registration address to have the details changed, again for a fee. All thoroughbreds have had these in place all the time, but it is comparatively new legislation for all others.

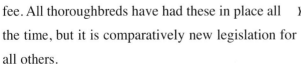

Your horse must have a passport

Vetting will not check on such things as being good to shoe or good in traffic.

VICES

Weaving is when the horse stands swaying, moving his weight from one foreleg to the other. Often noticed when the horse is excited in his stable. It is considered to put a lot more strain on the horses forelegs.

Crib biting is the act of taking hold of the door/fence with the teeth and tensing the neck muscles, drawing in air, which is known as **wind sucking**. A hard vice to stop, and horses with this problem are often lacking condition as their stomachs are full of air. There has been recent research into this vice, which suggests the cause may be stomach ulcers, not boredom.

Box walking, as the name suggests, means that the horse has much less rest than average, and finds it hard to settle when stabled.

Biting and kicking The majority of horses will have the odd nip when provoked, especially when having the girth fastened, and very fit horses are more prone to this. It becomes a vice when the normal reaction of the horse is to threaten to bite or kick people as soon as they approach.

As with any vice, with the correct management it is not a problem, but one to be avoided if you are not sure you could cope.

Subsequent costs will be for regular worming, which is often done at the same time on big yards. All horses have a relatively low level of worm burden, which does not cause a problem, but high levels can cause loss of condition, and even death, so regular worming is important. The worm eggs mostly come from the horse eating the immature larvae, which will be on the grass in the field. The main types of worms are redworm, whiteworm and tapeworm.

Bots flies lay eggs, often yellowish, on the horse's legs, then the horse licks them off and swallows them. It would take a whole chapter to explain this subject in detail. You will need advice about which wormer to use. Expect to be asked to worm your horse if you change to a new yard.

A livery yard owner I know, Lynda, falls into hysterical laughter when worming is mentioned and always recites the following conversation with a conscientious new owner about to worm her horse.

Owner: (won't give her name as she may read this) *'I am having a problem worming my horse, can you help?'*

Lynda: *'Of course, what's the problem?'*

Owner: *'I'm using a paste in a syringe but he keeps threatening to kick.'*

Lynda: *'He shouldn't be able to kick if you are by his head. Keep the syringe on his tongue and he should swallow the paste.'*

Owner: *'Oh dear, I thought it had to go in where the worms come out!'*

Teeth will need examining annually and probably require rasping. This ensures that the horse's teeth are as level as possible on the grinding surface, an important aspect to aiding digestion. An older horse will possibly need attention more often. If the horse had a tooth problem, or cannot grind his food properly, he could gradually starve to death! Being undershot or overshot are serious faults and need careful management.

If he is registered with a breed society or an association there will be a charge to transfer ownership.

Regular shoeing or trimming needs to be arranged. Again, register with a farrier as soon as you are definitely buying a horse. Farriers are extremely knowledgeable people and will often be able to help you out with any horse related queries. Feet need attention at least every 6-8 weeks, either shoeing or trimming, more often if you go on the road daily or there is a problem. Road studs can be used if you hack out a lot.

Daily grooming should include a check on the condition of the feet and shoes. It is very important to keep the horses feet balanced, a significant point in keeping your horse sound. Foot imbalance is a source of lameness, another reason to keep to a regular programme of foot care. If a horse needed remedial shoeing it will be more expensive and will need doing more frequently.

If your horse is going barefoot, as some horses are nowadays, they will need trimming every four weeks.

Neglecting foot care is cruel, and often done out of ignorance. This is a true story; a family fetched a pony on the yard as new livery clients, and on being asked who was their farrier, replied, 'Oh, we don't need one, the pony is already shod'.

Many alternative therapies are available for use with a horse, such as Reikki, Accupressure, Aromotherapy and many more. If using any of these, just check that the practitioners are recognised by the appropriate governing body.

Many injuries to horses benefit from physiotherapy treatment. They can benefit from ultra sound and massage as much as humans. This will be carried out by an equine physiotherapist, who will have initially trained as a human physiotherapist, then specialised in horses. Most physiotherapists work closely with vets, to produce the best result as quickly as possible. This can sometimes be claimed on the insurance, but not always.

I hope you will never have to use isolation procedure for your horse, except if it is a condition of the first week on a new yard. Some yards have this in place as a matter of routine for new arrivals.

Isolation is necessary if your horse has a contagious disease, to control the spreading of an outbreak. Each horse will need a specific person to care for him, who will take stringent precautions, such as having a change of clothing each time after treating the horse, disinfection of boots and the burning of any bedding removed from the stable. All grooming kit and feed bowls will need constant disinfecting. If there is an outbreak of strangles or equine influenza on a yard, it can be an extremely stressful time for all concerned, as there will be several horses needing isolation at the same time. Keeping each horse's equipment separate is even more important at this time. Care needs to be taken to prevent non essential people from moving around the stables near the isolation boxes.

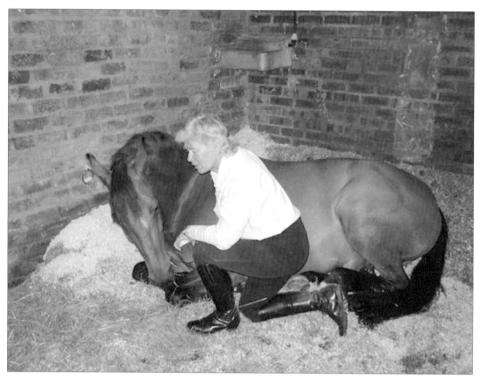

Sick nursing is another aspect I hope you never have to be involved with. The importance here is that the horse will need constant monitoring, and you will be carrying out the vet's instructions. Food and water will need to be offered in small quantities. The horse may not want to eat for a while, and picking fresh grass for him, or grating carrots may be the only way to tempt him to eat anything. He will need keeping warm, and may require different lightweight rugs, rather than one heavy one. He will be weak following an illness, and need careful management to return to full fitness again.

To learn more about alternative equine therapies and practitioners, you could visit www.reikihealersandteachers.net,

5
INSURANCE

"Do read the small print thoroughly to obtain the insurance you need." - A plea from vets, who deal with situations where owners find themselves with bills for thousands of pounds that are not covered by insurance

"I saw a pony in a field that in my opinion needed urgent vet attention. Because the owner was not available I got the vet to come and treat it, but I was liable for the bill as I had arranged the call out and the owner would not have called the vet." - Frances, caring owner on the same yard.

"Take care to mark your tack and belongings, and keep to well-established standards of husbandry with your horses to minimise the risks of injury." -

A plea from insurance companies

Remember that riding is classed as a high-risk sport

Your vet may recommend an insurance company as they will know which ones are best to deal with. I believe some companies fight each claim, whilst others are more realistic.

Third party public liability is essential, to cover any damage or incident caused by your horse, even though it may have got out of a well-fenced field with the gate still closed. You are still liable, even though you were not negligent. Two legal rulings have been made over the past two years, that reinforce this situation.

Household policies will not necessarily provide cover for your pet horse, so do check. Third Party insurance is part of the British Horse Society Gold membership.

All policies will expect you to follow accepted standards of welfare for your horse. Some may have a proviso such as insisting your horse has an annual dentistry or veterinary inspection.

One insurance company does not insure tack if it is kept at a yard with more than five stables. This fact is in the small print, so it does need reading.

Study the insurance policy in detail, as one person who helped in the research for this book found to her horror that her horse was not covered for third party liability, although she had presumed that the cover under 'Table A' in the policy, covering dressage and hacking, would automatically cover third party. She had been without that cover for four years, and thank goodness had not been involved in any incidents. Speak to other horse owners to see what experiences they have had with different companies.

Vet's fees can run into thousands if your horse is very ill or has an accident, so this cover is strongly recommended.

Transport insurance is a subject to be very aware of, so check if your horse is insured when travelling in a horsebox, either your own, or even if you are accepting a lift from a friend who is not charging you anything. Commercial transporters will have their own insurance, but do check private arrangements.

Some insurance will cover disposal costs, not a nice subject, but one that must be faced if you intend to keep the horse forever.

Check the excess amount on your policy, which varies with different companies. Just as important, check if the cover is for each incident or each year! In the event of your horse needing a general anaesthetic, you must first notify the insurance company before the horse is treated, so always keep the number at hand.

A colleague of mine who is an insurance broker has asked me to mention that many avoidable accidents happen due to ignorance or carelessness.

Some situations that can lead to serious accidents, but are avoidable with some knowledge

Always tie the horse so that there is a small loop of string between the lead rope and tie ring. This could be cut, or break under excessive strain in an emergency situation. Do not tie directly to anything that could break off if the horse pulled back. The fact that the attached object was still at the end of the rope would, to the horse, be perceived as a 'thing' following him, so he would run even faster to get away from the object.

It has been seen for a horse to be tied to the wing mirror on a horse box, an accident waiting to happen, or worse still to a loose drainpipe! A rail can be easily pulled and break off if a horse was tied to it. It's essential that the horse is tied to a solid

object, with a piece of string that could break in an emergency.

A friend of mine who is a very experienced instructor has seen a pony tied to a pram!

This same instructor mentioned about accidents she has come across or heard about with schooling aids being applied either too tightly or wrongly used, causing the horses to panic because they could not move easily. A horse with his head held tightly will often rear, and could fall over backwards. Very dangerous. It is vital to get help from a professional person, who understands the principle of the various gadgets and can show you how to use them to produce the desired result.

One common mistake that is made, with potentially very serious consequences, is tying a horse up with a very long rope, so that the horse could step over the slack. The rope could then tangle around the leg, causing the horse to fight and try and get away from the constriction! It can cause a severe wound to the leg, taking months to mend.

The other situation that can arise through ignorance is when horses are taken from a group in a field and just one horse is left on his own. He may crash through a gate or fence to follow his companions.

If a claim is made for any reason, the insurance company may refuse to insure that part of the horse again. For example, if there was a problem with the right fore leg, that leg would be excluded after the treatment had finished or if the horse suffered from a bout of lamintis, a chronic foot inflammation. This could prove expensive if the same leg became a problem again. Do check this with the company before you take out the policy, and take time to read the small print so that there is no misunderstanding about the level of cover.

Some companies do not cover the cost of the daily stabling at a veterinary hospital or remedial shoeing, both these costs can spiral if the problem is chronic. Another point to consider is transport if the horse becomes ill, will the insurance cover this, for several vet visits if needed. If not, this expense must be taken into the overall account.

Death and theft usually come with third party cover policies, and you may need to produce the receipt for the purchase price over a certain value.

Take photos of your horse from both sides and any markings, blemishes, marks etc, preferably one photo in summer and another in his winter coat, so in the extreme case of him going missing you have them to hand.

Some companies require a veterinary certificate of soundness before they will insure the horse. Other options will include **loss of use**, when you state what job your horse was bought for and if it cannot carry out that job because of injury or disease, you will receive some money if the horse is put down, or part payment if you keep it. It will mean that the horse has a freeze mark 'L' for loss of use. The onus will be on you to prove that the horse was capable of carrying out the activity

71

before the loss of use was claimed.

If you increase the value of your insurance, you will need to supply proof of why it is now more valuable than originally.

If your horse is to be ridden by **anyone else**, especially as a working livery, do arrange to have this fact part of your cover. Remember to check with insurers if there is someone else riding your horse if you are on holiday etc, or even if your friend occasionally rides the horse. It is a good idea to advise any other riders to take out a Personal accident policy. Many companies now offer this cover for non-owners.

Insurance cover for older horse can be limited, check with the different companies. Companies are often reluctant to set up a new policy for a horse aged over 15; others restrict the cover to **accident only** for older horses. Some insurance companies now offer a veteran horse policy for horses over 15 years up to 29 (sometimes older). Under such a policy, veterinary fees cover will be limited to accidents only, death of horse through accident only and there will be no loss of use option.

You can have a **freeze mark** put onto your horse, which is done by applying an extremely ice cold brand to the skin, so the hair follicles die off and the hair grows back white. You will then be recorded as the owner and if it were stolen it could be traced. If you buy a freeze marked horse, you can re register it in your name, for a fee, and presuming it was not stolen! This is quite a good deterrent to would be thieves.

Another security service available is micro chipping. Many horses will have this as part of their passport. This is under the skin and needs a scanner to read the number, whereas freeze marks are visible.

Do remember to mark your tack with your postcode, so if it were lost it would be identifiable. It can be marked by engraving on the stirrup bar, or with indelible ink under the saddle flap.

Check the type of lock needed to secure your tack room, as some companies stipulate this, e.g. five lever mortise locks as minimum. It may be a condition of insurance that the tack room is burglar alarmed.

If you do have a trailer, one recommended form of identification is to have your postcode put on the roof in very large letters, which will not come off.

Becoming a member of an Affiliated riding club or the British Horse Society will give you some insurance cover, so it is worth finding out what is on offer.

Tack can be covered, but do check to see where it may be kept! Some policies will only cover if the tack is at home, but sometimes your tack will be under household cover. It often will not be covered at a livery yard unless the insurer has agreed it in writing. One insurance company will only cover tack at a yard if there is someone in permanent residence on site. Others may have different restrictions, so it is very important to study the whole policy before deciding the degree of cover that you need.

You will also need accident cover for yourself!

6
WELFARE

"So many of our cruelty cases are caused through ignorance" - Inspector of a horse welfare charity.
"We want to return the pony you sold us, all its hair is falling out!" - Ignorant new owners, unaware that ponies moult in the spring.

It is essential that you have a reasonable knowledge of horse care before you become an owner. Many heartaches and sleepless nights are caused by inexperience, creating tension and problems all round for the horse and owner and possibly the family. If the pony is for a child, parents will need to be knowledgeable, or keep the pony at a place where there is supervision for the pony's welfare. A tiny puncture wound could go unnoticed and fester, and if not treated the same day could become serious, or the horse could be ill. Many children would not notice this, whereas adults would be more aware as they groomed the horse. You need a fair amount of knowledge so that you can monitor the condition and behaviour of your horse, even though someone else is looking after it.

It would be a good idea to weigh/measure your horse each month to check if he is getting fatter or thinner. You can do this with a piece of string, knotted, or a weight tape, which measures around the girth. Most horses in regular work become quite muscular, and stay at the same weight, but it is still wise to monitor his weight all year round. You may need advice on the ideal weight for your particular horse.

Becoming too fat can put undue strain on the joints, becoming too thin can cause lethargy or the horse not being able to carry out the job he was bought for, or even becoming a welfare issue.

Any one can get in touch with the RSPCA or ILPH to report a case of neglect and the officers are then sent to investigate the report.

If there is cause for concern the officers will offer advice in most cases and then monitor the case on a regular basis. One of the most often reported situations involve the horses' feet, as neglect for a relatively short time can lead to permanent damage and movement of the bones in the foot, and damage to the tendons, very painful. This can often cause the horse to be immobile and not be able to graze as it should, with subsequent weight loss. Other cases involve malnutrition; a horse can be on reasonable grazing, but have damaged teeth or mouth and therefore not able to eat and is being slowly starved.

I was once very concerned about a thin pony I saw in a field and I asked a welfare officer if he would investigate the circumstances. It turned out that the owners were very irate when approached, insisting that the daughter fed the pony a bucket full of food morning and evening. She did - a bucket full of hay, not much more than a handful! It actually needed half a bale of hay a day.

In extreme cases the owner could be invited to sign the horse over to the RSPCA or ILPH or be prosecuted for cruelty. If the horse is signed over they will treat and eventually re home the horse, with the society remaining the owner. If you were very worried about a particular horse that you knew, the officers would be able to give advice.

A different source of guidance?

Another experienced owner had bought a horse that was not very good physically. Although he was sound, he was very thin and lacked muscle and strength, but as they were experienced horse owners already they could see his potential. He did not thrive as expected, despite the best of attention for several months. As a last resort they held a prayer meeting in his field and they are sure that he began to improve from that day. He then developed into a successful competition horse, ridden by their daughter in many spheres, and lived to a ripe old age!

General notes on feeding

- A horse cannot be sick, so any wrong food is serious!
- A horse's stomach is only the approximate size of a rugby ball, and horses are naturally trickle feeders so that digestion is taking place most of the time. This is why they need mostly bulk food.
- Bulk food means grass or hay or haylage.
- Concentrates mean mixes, nuts, sugar beet or straights (barley, oats)
- A horse will need approximately 2.5% of his bodyweight in food per day; the best way to establish the weight is to ask a vet or experienced person for an educated guess! (see appendix for equation)
- A constant supply of fresh water is essential.
- The amount of feed needs monitoring to ensure the work and feed balance is working, this probably needs experienced assistance in the first few months.
- Changes in food needs to take place over at least ten days, as the bacteria in the gut need to change to be able to digest the different food efficiently.
- Keep to a routine as far as possible, to avoid the horse becoming fretful.
- Obviously keep feed bowls and buckets clean.
- Allow the stabled horse access to grass on a regular basis. If this is not possible, provide succulents such as carrots, turnips, swedes, or nets of collected grass.(But NOT grass mowings, which will start to ferment as soon as they are cut and would easily cause colic)

If the horse is suddenly not going to have the normal workload, cut out or reduce the concentrate foods and replace them with bulk.

- Maintenance – not being worked at all.
- Light work - an hours hacking most days, more at weekends.
- Medium work – more active work including jumping/dressage competitions and the work needed to become fit.
- Hard work – Hunting. One day eventing and Show jumping at affiliated level.
- Very hard - Three day eventing, racing -Endurance long distance riding

Types of feed in regular use

Cubes or nuts; these are prepared feeds that have been made into a cube form, so are easy to use. They are available in differing levels of nutritional value, so whichever type of diet your horse needs there will be a cube form. Sufficient vitamins and minerals for a healthy horse will have been added to the cubes, so nothing extra should be needed.

Mixes; these will be the same constituents as the cube form, but you can see the different feeds in the mix. Again, they are available as above, but usually more expensive.

Straights; these are the cereals on their own and if fed in quantity they will need to be supplemented by the appropriate vitamins or minerals to give a balanced diet.

Chop is a term given to hay or straw chopped into fine pieces, sometimes fed on its own, or often mixed with molasses and added minerals.

Sugar beet is mostly sold as shreds, which need soaking for a few hours before feeding, or cubes, that need twenty four hours to soak. Both of these could cause choking if fed in any quantity dry, as they would absorb the saliva in the mouth and throat. It is essential that you can recognise the difference between these cubes and the normal ones. Sugar beet flakes are now on the market, and they only need a few minutes soaking.

Most people use a scoop to measure the amount of food, so it is very important to weigh the different kinds of feed, as a scoop of cubes will weigh differently from a scoop of chop. It is important to know how much in weight your horse is receiving.

Hay is grass cut and allowed to dry on the field, then baled and stored.

Meadow hay is when the grass on a permanent pasture is left to grow long then cut. There is a wide variety in the quality and types of grasses in differing pastures, many having herbs in the mix. This kind of hay is the most usual.

Seed hay is where the grass is grown from seed as a crop, and will be higher in nutritional value, as only grasses that are wanted are grown.

Haylage is grass cut and allowed to wilt, then baled and vacuum wrapped in a plastic covering before it has dried out. The grass ferments. It needs to be used within a few days of the bale being unwrapped. It is more nutritious than hay, but has a higher water content, and is therefore heavier. Because of this more in weight will be needed than hay; be aware that the horse will be receiving more nutrition.

Straw is the stems left after combining cereals and is normally used as bedding. Occasionally oat straw is used as chop.

Feeding is an enormous subject, but if in doubt, keep the roughage as the main food source. There are plenty of books on feeding, just stick to manufacturer's recommendations. If you need to change a horse's feed it is best to stick to another type in the same brand, as a lot of the base food will be the same, a good point in preventing any digestive problems when changing the diet.

All the leading brands of feed manufactures are continuously researching the subject and adapting their feeds if necessary. They will all have a helpline manned by experienced nutritionalists, who will help you with any feeding queries.

Poisonous Plants

Something that you will need to familiarise yourself with is the recognition and identification of poisonous plants. Some are acutely dangerous, such as yew, which will cause death within a very short time, and others are toxic and build up over months, such as ragwort in its dried or wilted state.

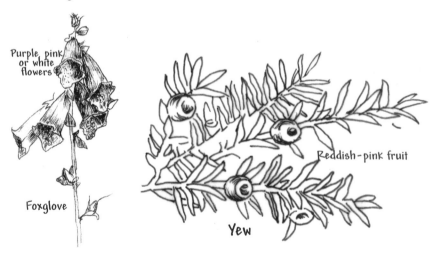

Purple, pink or white flowers

Foxglove

Reddish-pink fruit

Yew

FOXGLOVE	**YEW**
This is not usually eaten whilst it is growing, but would be a problem if it is wilting, when it would be eaten.	Very dangerous if eaten, as it will probably cause death before any treatment can be started.

RAGWORT

Poisonous if eaten in small quantities over a period of time, Ragwort causes liver failure, an untreatable condition. Horse tend not to eat it whilst it is growing, unless they are extremely hungry, which is why you can see it in fields. As soon as it wilts for any reason, it becomes palatable and will be eaten, which is why it is dangerous in hay. The majority of field owners pull it up and then burn it. Ragwort has become so prevalent that there is now a Ragwort Act 2003, as well as the Weeds Act 1959, which gives local authorities power to take action against owners of land full of ragwort.

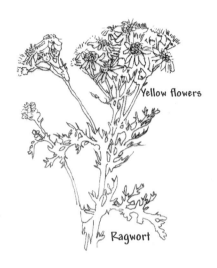

Yellow flowers

Ragwort

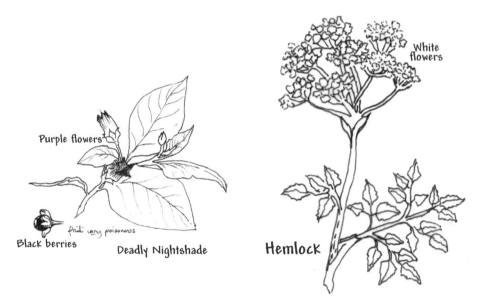

White flowers

Purple flowers

Black berries

fruit very poisonous

Deadly Nightshade

Hemlock

DEADLY NIGHTSHADE and **HEMLOCK** can be found in hedgerows, so this just stresses the importance of checking fields before horses are put into them

81

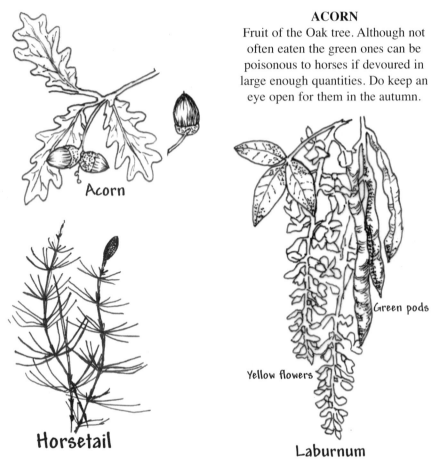

ACORN
Fruit of the Oak tree. Although not often eaten the green ones can be poisonous to horses if devoured in large enough quantities. Do keep an eye open for them in the autumn.

Acorn

Green pods

Yellow flowers

Horsetail

Laburnum

RHODODENDRUM, LAUREL and **LABURNUM** are often found in gardens, so they need fencing off from any proximity to horses. **PRIVET** is a hedge which should not be part of a field as it is also poisonous if eaten. Privet hedge cuttings would be the most dangerous. **BRACKEN** can be poisonous, but is seldom eaten, but in a drier state is toxic.

There are other poisonous plants, so especially if you will be having your horse at home, this subject will have to be on your list.

Poisoning in horses is not common, but can have effects that only become

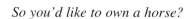

apparent in the long term, so can occasionally be the cause of inexplicable problems. Signs of poisoning would not often show at first, but unusual behaviour or loss of co-ordination should receive veterinary attention straight away.

Hunger will tend to make horses eat plants they normally would not touch. Should you acquire a field of your own, it is vital that you know about these plants. If other horses have lived in these fields for years there will not be a problem. Seed merchants or agricultural merchants will be able to put you in touch with someone who will have the knowledge to check your field.

You could test yourself to see if you are familiar with common ailments, such as

• Laminitis

This is where the fleshy part of the inside of the foot, the sensitive laminae, becomes inflamed and it is very painful and serious, needing very urgent attention. An affected horse will stand trying to keep his weight on the hind feet as the heel area of the front ones are so painful. Even when he recovers, the chances of this recurring are high. Some severe cases will not recover, so another reason to keep a check on your horse's condition. The feet are often left with very distinct rings around them, a sign to be aware of when horse viewing. It is a condition that can be managed, but not ideal.

• Thrush

A condition caused by a failure to clean out the horse's feet thoroughly, especially when he is stabled. An infection starts down by the side of the frog, is not detected and consequently the infection develops and will cause lameness, as a moist warm condition is ideal for bacteria to thrive. It is essential to clean right down by the side of the frog, a point often missed.

• Ringworm

A fungal condition which causes scaly patches on the skin where the hair drops off, but the surrounding area is still affected. This can be transferred to humans, and is very contagious. Horses having this need to be isolated and stringent care taken till it has cleared up, to prevent it spreading.

- **Colic**

Stomach ache in the horse. A horse cannot be sick, so any digestive problem is serious. A horse restless, lying down, then rolling, getting up and kicking at his flank are all danger signs and need expert help urgently. Initial symptoms are similar, and it could be a sign of indigestion, where a muscle relaxant will cure the problem, or it could be the first signs of a blockage or worst of all a twisted gut. These last two are very serious, so do call out a vet, as prompt treatment can make a big difference to the eventual outcome.

- **Colds**

Horse has a runny nose and cough. Always take his temperature. If the nasal mucous is green, it could be Strangles.

- **Strangles**

The horse has a high temperature and develops an abscess under his throat that will eventually burst and need treating as a wound. Serious cases take weeks to recover and occasionally can be fatal. An outbreak of strangles would send out alarm bells to all your neighbouring horse owners, as it is very contagious and can spread just by someone patting your horse, then afterwards going to visit another. Responsible yard owners simply stop all horse movement in and out till the outbreak dies down, which could be several weeks.

- **Sweet itch**

An allergic reaction to midge bites. A horse suffering from this condition will need careful management. He will be scratching against anything he comes into contact with. A severe case will make your horse's life a misery. But there are rugs and

hoods to help alleviate the symptoms. He will need keeping stabled during the daytime, from early morning when the midges begin to appear till late evening. He can be turned out at night time, but you will have to be an early riser.

- **Sunburn**

Some horses with white on their muzzle may develop scabs, but high factor sunscreen can help!

When to call the vet, urgently! Always have the number handy

(remember that if a general anaesthetic is needed, the insurance company must be notified beforehand)

- Any wound that is spurting blood.
- Any wound on a joint where the skin has been broken. Clear fluid from a joint is serious, because if the joint becomes infected it will be disastrous.
- Any injury to the eyeball.
- Any large tear, as if it needs stitching it is important to do it straight away to stand the best chance of healing easily.
- Severe lameness, when the horse is unable to put weight on his leg.
- Sweating, without having been working, Sweating in these cases is a sign of pain, not a sign of hard work. It can be a sign of azoturia (tying up) if it happens very soon after a fit horse begins working and his whole body stiffens up and he can hardly move.
- A high temperature. Usually taken because the horse is not eating, has a discharge from his nose, or distressed breathing.
- Constantly lying down and getting up again, maybe rolling.
- Choking.
- Difficulty in breathing, sides heaving.

So you'd like to own a horse?

It is essential that you know the postcode of the yard, and any direction advice to help a locum vet find you quickly. An Ordnance Survey grid reference will help.

Some 'horsey expressions' that may help you.

If you know them all, great!

Aids - The signals that you give to the horse to explain what you wish him to do.

Blood horse - A thoroughbred.

Cast - When a horse has rolled, jammed his legs against the wall and can't get up.

Dishing - A fault in leg action, where the foreleg is thrown outwards as well as forwards.

Entire - Another word for stallion.

Favouring a leg - When the horse does not put his full weight on one of his limbs. An indication of lameness.

Galvaynes groove - A mark on the tooth, which can be used in assessing the ageing of the horse.

Hogged mane - When the mane is clipped off.

Inscisors - The biting teeth. These are also the teeth used to ascertain the age of the horse.

Jenny - A female donkey.

Kimblewick - A type of curb bit.

Lockjaw - Another name for tetanus.

Mule - A cross between a female horse and male donkey. Mules are infertile.

Nearside - Left hand side.

Offside - Right hand side.

Poisonous plants - You will need to be familiar with these, as access to them can prove disastrous. *See pages 80 - 82*

Quidding - The horse drops food from his mouth as he is chewing, - *Bad sign*.

Rig - Term used to describe a male horse that has not been gelded successfully. These can be extremely disruptive as they will look like a gelding but have the traits and behaviour of a stallion.

St Christopher - Patron saint of travellers, who used to be mainly horsemen.

To take hold - When the horse is taking the bit and pulling against the rider. Not nice!

Up to weight - This describes a horse whose build can carry his rider with ease.

Voltige - Acrobatic exercises on horseback, the horse on the lunge. Usually young people vaulting on and off.

Weight calculation - Girth squared x length from point of shoulder to point of buttock, divided by 300, gives approx weight in pounds.

Xenophon - A famous Athenian soldier and horseman c450 BC, whose writings about the principles of riding and horsemanship are still relevant in many cases.

Youngster - Usually unbroken.

Zoonoses - Diseases that can be spread from horses to humans, such as ringworm and Weils disease.

If you do not understand any of them, find out before you set out on the quest for a horse.

Abbreviations

TB means thoroughbred

PC will mean Pony Club.

RC will mean Riding Club

ID is Irish Draught

PBA is Part bred Arab

Anglo means crossed with a TB.

Picking out feet

Learn to identify everyday pieces of equipment and tack. You will need to be competent at catching, grooming, pulling manes, picking out feet etc, so that the horse does not receive any nervous vibes from you.

There are many monthly magazines full of articles on all aspects of equestrian life. Many of these will be subjects relevant to the welfare of the horse, and will be of interest to horse owners.

Collect some books to study, the Manual of Horsemanship, published by the Pony Club, will cover all basic subjects.

There are hundreds on the market, but stick to just a few to avoid confusion. There is a series

of booklets that each describes a different section of horse care such as grooming, poisonous plants, travelling. They will be available from most large saddlers.

If you are not absolutely confident of caring for your new horse, keep him with an experienced person who is willing to help you, for the first few months, even if it is more expensive.

A welfare point to bear in mind is what will you do if the horse is no longer needed, either through circumstances, being outgrown, or problems causing the horse becoming non-rideable? Decide before you buy if you intend to sell or re home him when he is outgrown or no longer needed.

A horse is a very expensive pet and it is often in the horse's better interest to be sold on to another home than trying to keep him in difficult circumstances. Be aware that it may not be easy to re-home a horse quickly, especially if he has not been ridden or schooled regularly. For a horse to be saleable it must be safe for people to come and try him out, so must be in regular work.

If a pony is outgrown, often word of mouth can find him another home, or you can advertise him, and check that the people interested will look after him as well as you have.

Your horse may live for 30 years after you buy him, and will still need caring for in his old age.

The Animal Welfare Act of 2006 has introduced a clause whereby a welfare officer can issue an Improvement Notice if he considers an animal is not receiving basic welfare care. All owners have a duty of care to provide adequate shelter, grazing and water for the horse, and keep him safe.

The majority of equine welfare societies operate under the umbrella of the National Equine Welfare Council.

These photographs show 'Cariad' at 6 years old and 36 years old, still well and sound! His rider in the photo still rides him gently twice a week!

As long as you find the best home for him, the horse will usually settle with new owners, as he settled with you. If you decide to keep him forever, it will then be your decision, usually with a vet, when to have him put down. Old horses can be very expensive to keep, the insurance cover for veterans is usually minimal and only for accidents, so does not cover fees for illness or problems with joints etc. It can run into hundreds of pounds for an attack of colic or digestive problem, and could be up to thousands for the very serious twisted gut, which always needs surgery to stand a chance of recovery, and could have a long period of recovery.

If you put a horse out on loan, do have a watertight agreement, so you have the final say if need be. It is vital that you visit the new home and check out where he will be kept, and how experienced the new owners are. Occasionally loaners have lost track of their horses, only to find out that they have been sold on. On the other side I know of horses that have been put out on loan and the original owner

90

to disappear and never enquire after the horse again!

If the horse has an incurable illness or a poor quality of life it is often in his best interest to have him put down, then you know that he ended his life peacefully. Once you sell your horse you will have no control over his life.

A cost that must be faced is disposal if your horse dies. Currently this is a few hundred pounds, and there are only a few abattoirs that are licensed to take horses. The cost may be met by the insurance, but do check. If you wished the horse to be cremated and want to keep the ashes, some abattoirs will provide this service. There are pet burial grounds that take horses and provide a place for remembrance.

A point that also comes under the heading of welfare, is to be constantly on the lookout for any rubbing or pressure caused by rugs slipping back onto the withers, or straps chafing. If leg straps broke, a rug would slip round and cause the rug to pull sideways.

Badly fitting tack can be painful and cause many problems, so keep an eye on the horse's condition, as if he changes shape the tack may need altering.

The ILPH, BHS and RSPCA all have welfare helplines and have a countrywide net of officers. They are there, together with the other organisations, to offer any advice you may need on any welfare issue.

In icy weather someone will have to be in charge of breaking the ice on frozen water supplies, and carrying water to the horses if needed! Obviously extra hay needs to be given to field horses if the ground is frozen.

Pony Club games need skill and concentration

7
CLUBS, COMPETITIONS and COURSES

"Hubby, kids, ponies and bike all pack up for a show at weekend; son hates ponies but loves his bike, meets his pals on the showground, Hubby drives us there then reads the paper or sneaks off to chat to other dads, I polish the ponies, girls ride them. Keeps us all out of mischief"   Pony Club Mother.
"We plan to go to one show every month from April to October and even if we don't win it is a good day out. Winter time we stay at home!" - A group of owners from the same livery yard, who enjoy each others company and their love of horses.

My friend used to compete before she was married and when her children were small they came riding and she was happy to watch them on their lessons and in any little competitions that the riding school put on. Occasionally dad fetched them, but as he had no interest in horses, he stayed in the car and insisted that they came home the instant the ride finished, and never watched them ride. When the inevitable happened and the girls were ready for a pony, dad's comment was *'as long as I am not involved'*

The first day they came to look after the new pony, dad came to *'see what I've spent my hard earned money on,'* even though he still had no idea why anyone would want to have large, smelly pony that needed brushing for hours, then went into the field and rolled in the mud to get dirty again. By the end of the week he was carrying in the tack and grooming kits and commented that he had not realised how friendly ponies can be. Week two saw him brushing the pony, and to cut a long story short, 12 months later he was driving the car and trailer to shows and became a stalwart of the local Riding Club committee! …Dads beware…!

Sherrifmuir Highland ponies with their riders, enjoying a day out on a pleasure ride

Pony Club Centre members and instructors after taking tests at a rally.......

For children there is the national Pony Club, whose local branches arrange rallies, tests and competitions at different levels, and has been the grounding place for many of present day top class competitors. Many current Pony Club members will go on to become famous riders!

BHS and ABRS Approved Riding Schools can now run Pony Club Centres for children without their own horses and be part of their local National Pony Club.

This is the breeding ground for many potential owners, and a well run riding school will produce riders capable of being excellent owners. These riders may take part in every type of riding and horse care, but their sound foundation and knowledge will stand them in good stead. Just as important, the horses that they have should be in competent hands.

The British Riding Clubs have groups in all counties. Being a member, child or adult, gives you the opportunity to meet like minded people, compete in a wide range of shows and activities, and take part in social events and training courses.

There are regular newsletters and most clubs send teams to compete in all disciplines, and attend events on a national level. British Riding Club and Pony Club qualifications are recognised by the British Horse Society as on a level with their Stage exams.

These clubs all have an **annual subscription fee**, with entry fees being paid for classes and courses. A pre requisite of being a club member is often that you will be asked to do a duty day. This means helping at the shows, setting up or stewarding or any job going. Both Pony Club and Riding Club committee members would welcome help from parents or friends of competitors, as the manpower at shows is voluntary, a point to always bear in mind. Club uniform sweatshirts, ties and baseball caps are normally offered for sale by these clubs, not essential, but often bought.

A pre requisite of being a club member is often that you will be asked to do a duty day

The cost of transport to the events will have to be considered, as will extra tack and equipment. Competing at affiliated events will mean that you have to become a member and then register your horse with that discipline, usually on an annual basis.

For riders not wishing to attend formal competitions there are pleasure rides, 10 - 20 miles, often arranged by endurance riding clubs, so you could progress to endurance rides. (Hours and hours of fittening!)

Many riders don't want to take part in a structured group. Part of the enjoyment of horse owning is the fact that you can ride whenever you want, or change your mind and not be tied to time scales. Most areas will have farm rides, where you pay a fee to use the facilities, which usually include a track with optional fences of varying degrees of difficulty.

Also popular is a competition called Le Trec, combining map reading, cross country and schooling.

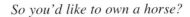

Try your hand at a different ways of riding such as western or side-saddle

Both Association of British Riding Schools and British Horse Society approved centres have proficiency type tests in riding and stable management, starting at a very basic standard and rising to a high level of competence, giving access to those associations exams. These are an excellent way of acquiring skills.

Even owning a horse may not be the end of paying for lessons, as many people enjoy the continuous progress and comradeship of lessons. Having lessons then being able to go home and practise your homework can be great fun. Regular training/coaching will benefit both you and your horse, whatever level you are at, and help the partnership reach it's full potential.

If you attend competitions, especially with children, at first choose a low-key venue, where they can enjoy taking part without undue pressure, until they wish to aim higher.

Many Riding Centres arrange specialist clinics on a regular basis, which you could attend if you enjoy training.

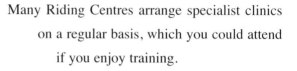

Within all these groups you could meet people with similar interests ....

The situation can arise where you enjoy the competitive side of horse owning so much that you end up competing most weeks and become hooked on going to events! Many first horses have given so much confidence to their riders that their skills have blossomed, causing the horse to become redundant as his capability does not grow to match that of the jockey. In this case a less strenuous life style for the horse could be called for and he would go on to give another rider confidence.

If competitions become part of your scene it can boost your riding budget quite a few notches, especially if you ride on a team, as this will entail a lot of extra training and travelling expense, as well as time. There is no limit to how high a standard you can reach!

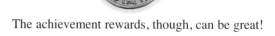

The achievement rewards, though, can be great!

8
ABILITY AND COMMITMENT

Some comments made in good faith by new owners-

"He is fast asleep with his legs resting on the wall" - The horse was cast!
"I am angry and going to send this pony back as all its hair is falling out". - True story! The pony was simply getting on with the annual moult in the spring.
"He is having a lovely run round on his own in here" - Owner sat on the gate watching her horse galloping flat out and whinnying as the other two horses had been taken out of the field, leaving him on his own in panic mode.

One major consideration in being an owner is the amount of time that you can set aside to enjoy your horse. Speak to others to find out how they arrange their time, as this is often the part that dictates the type of livery you choose. Time can fly just catching, grooming and chatting to the horse, before ever you tack up and ride. What used to be one hour's ride at a school will spread to cover three or four hours if you look after your own. Horses are very good listeners, nothing will shock them!

I know of riders who have helped other owners with their horses, becoming involved with the daily care and exercise. These situations have come through word of mouth or strategically placed adverts in livery yards/tack shops. Owners with two horses sometimes welcome help with the care, and you will quickly decide if you enjoy the hands on experience.

If you are not absolutely confident of caring for your new horse, keep him with an experienced person who is willing to help you for the first few months, even if it is more expensive.

Confidence is essential in handling, and will come with practice. Most horses enjoy being groomed and handled and it is very satisfying to have a nicely turned out horse, even though you know that if they go in the field their first task is to roll. Rolling is nature's way of keeping healthy, and at the end of the day, natural instincts always win! To keep the mane tidy it is pulled, that is the long hairs are pulled out leaving the shorter ones, and as they grow to become the long ones they are in turn pulled out. If this is done regularly, the mane will always look neat. The exception is a horse living out all the time, as he needs his mane for protection from the rain.

Take into account the time for tack cleaning, washing numnahs and rugs, and washing the horse's mane and tail. Travelling time to the stables must be taken into consideration, and maybe even the cost of fuel.

If you feel you need to gain experience, I would suggest that you offer to help out at a riding school or yard where there will be knowledgeable people to guide you. This way you will gain confidence in handling horses, which is crucial before becoming an owner. Don't be surprised if you are not welcomed with open arms at first, as newcomers to horse handling will need constant supervision, but if you show commitment you should become appreciated.

You will learn the basics of safe handling, such as how to tie up using a quick release knot, turn out a horse into the field safely and become capable of reading the horses' reactions to various situations and, very importantly, how not to have the lead rope when holding your horse, even a quiet one.

Quick release knot

Always have any spare rope looped across your hand NEVER wrapped around your hand. If the horse took fright over anything, or tripped you could be dragged!

An excellent way to acquire relevant knowledge would be to go on a BHS Horse Owners course. These courses are often run as night school classes at a college or Approved riding school. This is a mainly theoretical course, as it is assumed that if you are considering owning a horse, your practical skills will

already be sufficient. ABRS and BHS Approved schools offer Riding and Stable Management Tests to their clients, which cover all aspects of horse care.

A horse being handled by an inexperienced person will either worry and become anxious, or dominate you. As you learn to handle horses, they will understand what is needed from them, building up a mutual confidence. It is essential that you know how to tack up easily and be able to check that it is safe.

Now is the time to take a serious look at the pros and cons, which will lead to the choice of horse. **Your own ability** will dictate the starting point.

If you have already had plenty of experience in handling and riding lively horses, the pointers about having a quiet horse to start with will not be relevant, but the costs and commitment will be the same.

Even if you are very experienced already, a gentle disposition in a horse may be your priority, or you may be seeking an uncomplicated companion. Whichever is your choice the following tips should help you find the horse for you. It really is a decision that is very much dictated by how you personally relate to each horse.

- Are you at ease on a horse that tends to become lively or excited, could you calm him, or would you prefer a calmer mount?

- Could you cope easily with any quirks the horse may have (there are so many) or would you prefer a horse that is fairly straight forwards to handle?

- Can you recognise if a horse is high spirited or a bully or just anxious? If in doubt ask advice from your instructor and make clear your end goal.

These three actions often appear to be the same, but need different ways to deal with the situations. The basic standard will include being able to go into a field to catch your horse, groom him, recognise if he was off colour, care for his feet and tack him up safely. You should be able to spot any signs that he is not well, and know when to ask for assistance or a vet.

Knowing a horse's natural behaviour pattern and instincts is essential. If the horse is feeling dominant and not accepting you as his natural leader, big problems will arise. Refusal to be caught or tacked up can take all the pleasure out of riding.

Horses' natural instincts usually kick in when unexpected things arise, so you need experience in dealing with all situations that may present themselves. One example would be if a horse was tied up and standing quietly and a sudden loud noise occurred. A natural instinct would be to run away from anticipated danger, so the horse would swing around to look towards the noise, possibly want to flee a distance before confronting the perceived danger. As this is not possible, being tied up, some horses will pull back to try to get loose to escape. Not naughty, just scared. Another example is if the horse felt threatened by you whilst in a controlled space, he could not flee, so would resort to threatening to kick or bite.

Many horses feel secure in a group, but do not like to be on their own, which can be a big minus point, and is a problem that takes a lot of time and patience to overcome. Horses naturally follow the herd leader, so the leader has to be you!

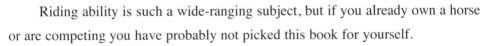

Riding ability is such a wide-ranging subject, but if you already own a horse or are competing you have probably not picked this book for yourself.

It is essential that you will have ridden a wide variety of horses to develop your horsemanship. Some you will have liked, some not, but all their differences will have helped develop your feel of how an experienced rider copes with all situations. It will also have started to give you ideas about the type of horse you would like to be riding and handling.

Hacking on the roads in all traffic will have helped, as unpredictable situations are more likely to occur at these times. Riding in the open, preferably with others, should hold no fears, and it goes without saying that you are secure and confident at walk, trot and canter, and able to decide when you wish to change speed.

If your interest is in hunting or more strenuous competitions, be aware of how much time needs to be set aside for riding to keep both of you fit.

A good idea would be to take the BHS Riding and Road Safety Certificate if you are going to be mainly hacking.

One major consideration in being an owner is having the time to set aside to enjoy your horse. Time can fly handling your horse, as there is so much to do every time you meet, besides the actual riding time. Speak to other owners, find out how they enjoy their horses and arrange the time they spend with them.

Be very practical about where your strengths and weaknesses lie, as being less than 100% confident with any animal is known to be a recipe for disaster. Gaining hands on experience will stand you in good stead before you own a horse!

9
CHOOSING THE HORSE

"Never buy a chestnut mare" - A regular statement made to horse buyers
"My best horses have been chestnut mares" - Peter, well known top class show jumper.

"Four white legs, keep him not a day,
Three white legs, send him far away,
Two white legs, give him to a friend,
One white leg, keep him to the end."   An old saying?

The author's favourite horse was a chestnut mare with four white stockings. (Well, second favourite, as my first horse, a palomino was always number one)

Once the decision has been made to buy a horse, set a financial limit that does not entail taking out a mortgage. It is best to assume that the cost may never be recovered, although this is not strictly so. Study adverts for the kind of horse you may be interested in, comparing the prices, which will have quite a range. Some prices may include tack, most will not. It is not possible to say how much a horse will cost, but looking around should give you a guideline. A horse that has been placed in competitions recently will command a higher price than one that has not, as will a horse with a good reputation.

Having spoken to many horse owners, all agree that the most important thing to be at the top of your list must be **temperament,** which can vary, irrespective of

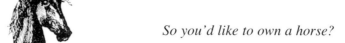

their age, breed or type. The horse's temperament must suit you and your lifestyle. Some are very active and need to be working very regularly to thrive, whilst others are happy working in a more casual manner.

'My priority for a horse was that I could trust him with my children' was one comment I received from many parents, and Jackie added *'Even though there is always a chance of an accident with any horse, I knew it would not be caused by the horse misbehaving"*

Be aware that some horses, often with Arab or TB in their make up, become fit in less time than a more placid horse and will need more work to keep them happy. A quirky temperament can be manageable in very experienced hands, but must be the exception to the rule

I know a talented show jumper, a mare, so territorial in her stable that to catch her, the groom had to go into the next stable, lean over the wall, drop a rope over the horse's neck and then climb down into the box. Once the horse was caught she could be tied up and then she was ok. *'A brilliant mare'* was her owner's description of her, (not the grooms!). With those owners her quirk was not a problem, but for most people she would have been a no-no.

I once competed on a horse that was problematical to get on, but an excellent jumper when you were on board. My friend and I devised a routine to outwit the horse, and she came with me to the shows. My only problem was that I could only attend shows that she could come to! That horse went on to become a Grade B with a rider who only ever mounted by vaulting on board quick as a flash, so no problem for him. The attitude of many professional riders to strange temperaments and vices is *'I don't mind what he does in his spare time'*

The ideal is a stress free horse that will be caught, tied up, and groomed without any problems, and be fairly obedient when you ride him.

CHECKLIST

Height   *14.2/15.*
Age Range
Type
Sex   *G.*
Colour   *?*
Temperament
Behaviour
Degree of Training

Draw up a list to reinforce what the priorities are for your horse

Hacking leisurely

The horse must be good in traffic, alone or with a companion.

Hacking on pleasure rides

This will be in company. The horse needs to be ridden sufficiently to become fit enough, and be manageable when cantering along with other horses. If the rides are not local, boxing must be trouble free.

Endurance riding

The fitness level for you both will dictate the distances you undertake, and travelling well will be essential, as these events take place all over the country. Endurance riding is not for the faint hearted and you need good friends to 'crew' for you.

Jumping at home and pleasure rides

The horse should be confident tackling small straightforward jumps. You can introduce variety and height when you want to. Jumps on pleasure rides are usually natural fences. The horse should behave when following others.

Jumping at competitions; Clear round and Novice

The partnership needs to be confident at home at the height of the competitions at least, and preferably be at a higher level at home. Jumps with all colours of fillers should hold no fears. When looking at the schedules, check to see the **definition of novice**, as this can vary at different shows. Read the schedule to check the heights in the different classes, usually novice, intermediate and open.

Jumping competitively; Affiliated or Working Hunter

The point to establish at affiliated competitions, which will be under the rules of the BSJA is, has your horse won prize money? This will guide you as to the classes that you can take part in. The grading goes with the horse and it cannot be down graded, so make sure that the grade is correct for the level you want to compete at. There is a cost for registering the horse and yourself each year.

Working hunter classes are normally run by riding a course of natural looking fences, sometimes including bullfinches and ditches. The clear rounds go forwards to give a show, and be appraised on their conformation.

Dressage, schooling at home or on courses

During training, the riding needs to be structured, so you ride to improve the horse

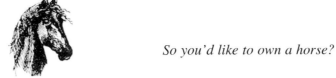

each time. Courses can be fun as well instructional, especially if you stay with the same trainer and develop a rapport. Ideally you need access to an arena to ride in.

Dressage, competing unaffiliated

Most riding clubs and training centres run dressage competitions, ideal for competing, and if you are placed and winning at this level it may be worth thinking of affiliating. Again, the horse must be a calm traveller, so you both arrive in a good mood.

Dressage, affiliated

You will need to become a member of British Dressage and register the horse with them. The grading system is based on points gained, the number of points determining the level at which the horse competes. Dressage differs from show jumping in that one can appeal to have the horse down graded if the rider is at a lower level (riders are categorised according to the level at which they have acquired points). The downgrading is only for the current rider, and will revert if the horse is ridden by anyone else, and you cannot take part in Championships.

Cross country

As with hunting, you both will need to be fit enough to minimise risk of injury by tiredness, but it can be exhilarating. All jumps are fixed, so you either go clear or risk a fall! Body protectors are compulsory, and you will wear a rugby type shirt, usually the same colours as your hat silk.

Eventing

This is a combination of dressage, show jumping and cross country and is the ultimate competition for competitive riders. Starts at riding club level, which is to quite a high level, and increases to British Eventing, where you have to register yourself and your horse There is a points system, and you move up the grades as points are gained. To complete all three sections in one day you will have to put in

an immense amount of work to become proficient in all three spheres. An added cost could be a second saddle and bridle and set of riding kit.

Hunting

The horse (and you) will need to follow a fitness programme so that the work involved will not tire the horse. Injuries often happen as a horse's muscles become tired, so the fitness must be maintained for the whole season; quite a tall order. There will be a subscription fee for the season, and if you are a visitor or occasional hunter there will be a charge, 'cap'. Fox hunting is banned, and hunts follow a scent, but you still need to be able to jump whatever fences appear, in a group.

Showing

Whatever the breed or type of your horse, there will be a class for him somewhere. When showing your horse in one of these classes, the manners, turnout and presentation will be a very important factor. Each horse/pony will be expected to give an individual display to show off his paces, and his turnout will need to be immaculate.

All Riding Clubs and Pony Clubs will have a wide variety of classes, and local shows will be advertised in feed stores and saddlers. It would take another book to list all the societies. Enquire from the breed societies about competitions for which your horse is eligible.

When the main jobs for your horse have been decided, if you wish to compete, go along to watch some competitions. (If you really want to go behind the scene, become a volunteer). This will give you an idea of the standard you need to be at in order to compete, You can also see the different types of horses that are taking part. Local affiliated riding clubs usually have a high standard, and a horse may come up for sale that has competed there so you will have an idea of its level of training.

Next, the actual horse

A good rule of thumb for a first horse is to decide what is the **main** purpose for which your horse will be used, then v**iew some that have already done that activity, even in a very limited way**.

Unless you are very experienced in training horses, or have daily contact with such a person, please do not even go to look at a horse that needs 'bringing on' or 'has potential' unless it has been ridden, even at a very basic level in **your main interest**. The time involved can be enormous and you need the knowledge to understand the problems that will arise and how to train the horse calmly and systematically. Almost daily training is necessary to train the horse in another discipline, or train him from scratch. I have met countless people who have viewed their new horse as a challenge and then come unstuck, with a bewildered horse, and frustrated owner. If you and your new horse both enjoy and feel comfortable in your chosen discipline, you can progress and that is where the benefits of being a horse owner will increase.

If the horse is going to be taken out and about for any reason he will need to be easy to load, behave whilst other horses are working around him, and preferably stay on the box quietly whilst the other horse unloads and leaves. Before you set sail to go viewing make a list of your preferences concerning:

- Height
- Age range
- Type
- Sex
- Colour
- Temperament
- Training/behaviour

Height may be an important factor if the horse or pony is going to compete. The height is taken from the ground to the withers and can be **measured in hands,** which is four inches, or ten centimetres, approximately a hand. Although traditionally a horse's height is referred to in hands, most schedules now use centimetres to categorise ponies into the different heights.

Conversion table:

12	hands	=122cm
12.2	hands	=128cm
13	hands	=133cm
13.2	hands	=138cm
14	hands	=143cm
14.2	hands	=148cm
15	hands	=153cm
15.1	hands	=155cm

(this is the height of a show cob)

Measuring the horse

It is usually considered to be a pony if the height does not exceed 14·2 hands and a horse is above that height, although there is now a large competitive group of ponies not exceeding 15 hands (153cms).

Check the rules in the sort of classes you are planning to enter to make sure the height is within the range. The Pony Club often uses the rider's age as a factor, where the height of the pony may not be as important, but Riding Clubs and affiliated competitions will have height/age combinations. For example a small child could have a 12 hh pony and be able to compete in lead rein classes for 12 hh ponies as well as 12.2 hh classes.

With height restriction classes, a horse or pony may need a life height certificate, which can only be given by a named vet in each area. Vets have a level piece of ground at their practise, on which the pony stands to be measured. The

horse or pony has to be six years old to have a life certificate.

On a practical level, you will need to be able to tack up and mount easily to avoid hassle. A pony that was sturdy enough for a parent to ride could be ideal in a family situation. Often ponies are sold as being outgrown, but a tall person can ride a smaller native type pony, as it is your weight that dictates the carrying ability of the pony, not your height.

Look at some of the riders in Mountain and Moorland classes, their legs reach the ponies knees, but the ponies are perfectly capable of carrying them. Watch a Pony Club gymkhana competition, those ponies are often small but more than capable of carrying their jockeys at speed.

One of the funniest sights I have seen recently was two adults taking part in a 'fun' charity competition for pairs dressage. Both were in full competition dress and very earnest, riding two **Shetlands**. The sight of all those legs going at top speed was hilarious. Joking apart, those little ponies were quite capable of taking the ladies' weight: the ponies were used as pack ponies in their native habitat. Shetland ponies are known to be the strongest breed in relation to size. They are referred to in inches for their height, not hands.

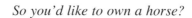

Falabellas are miniature horses and never referred to as ponies! They have excellent temperaments, make good pets and are often driven.

Falabella -
Looking Glass Baby Lourdes

Age Range

The horse needs to be trained, but often temperament is more important than age. Most horses are fully developed and know their jobs by the age of six and barring accidents and illness easily work for at least another 12-15 years without any signs of age creeping up. At my riding school there are several over 21 year olds, but you would not be able to tell by just looking at them.

Ex-show pony *Jubilee*, 25 years old and still enjoying being wanted.

Seven horses and ponies at the school came from competition homes, and had been kept fit and well by their knowledgeable owners. When their owners needed to re-home them, they chose a good riding school, as the horses would be well cared for, and their abilities would be appreciated as schoolmasters, to train the next generation of competitors!

Photo of *Shelly* jumping at 21years old, bought at three and now 30 years young!

Many elderly horses have many workable years left, and will be well trained. As old age creeps up it is essential to keep exercising gently and regularly.

The drawback maybe the age limits that insurance companies set, so that may well give you the age range.

Some youngsters have a calm temperament that is natural to them, others become livelier as they mature. Others remain lively or calm all their lives.

Type

Pure breds of any breed will have characteristics that may be on your checklist. If you want a pedigree, the breed societies often have a for sale list that could be worth looking at. Be aware that even if a particular breed is renowned for a certain trait, so much will depend on the individual horse's temperament, as well as how it was initially trained and how the previous owner handled and rode him.

The majority of horses do not have a pedigree and are of unknown breeding, so you have to look at the horse to make your decision about it.

A Cob is a type with a sturdy build and shortish legs, usually with feathers (the hair around the fetlock) They can range from being gentle hacks to successful competition horses. Their build makes them suitable for carrying light or heavier riders. Most cobs have smooth paces, making them popular rides. If they are shown in cob classes they usually have

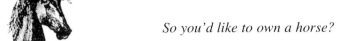

their manes hogged (which means that the mane is clipped off).

The Welsh Cob is a recognised breed, which keeps its mane, often with an extravagant knee and hock action, and if you get the chance to attend a County level show, the Welsh Cob in hand class is a must, with the cobs being shown by their enthusiastic handlers - a sight not to be missed!

Arabs are said to be the purest breed in the world, and most other breeds have an infusion of Arab blood somewhere in their history. Thoroughbreds are said to be able to trace there bloodlines back to three famous Arabs, The Byerley Turk, The Godolphin Arab and The Darley Arabian. They are renowned for their endurance and strength and are often used for endurance riding. If you own an Arab, you will have a beautiful, intelligent horse, that will need lots of exercise to keep him fit and happy.

Thoroughbreds are bred to race, and their stamina, speed and agility are renowned. This makes them much sought after for competitions such as eventing, where you need speed, agility and stamina, and show jumping where the same qualities can be channelled. Their agility and elegance help them in dressage, but their temperament can work against them if they become excited or confused. Thoroughbreds are known to be volatile at times, so to thrive they need to be in experienced hands.

Thoroughbred Sweet Chariot, originally raced and now achieving great success in Horse Trials

courtesy of Jo Prestwich

Traditionals: Always shown with full mane and feathers left in their natural state

courtesy of P. Tarne

British Native Breeds

Blackie and Brownie
(Shetland type)

SHETLAND: Up to 10.2 hh (42 inches) Black, bay, chestnut, coloured. Very sturdy. Temperament said to be independent. These two also drive successfully.

Honey Rose
of Mitchelland

HIGHLAND: 13.2-14.2hh. Dun, grey, black. Broad chested and sturdy, with full mane and tail. Temperament said to be placid and intelligent

Escowbeck Eddie

DALES: 13.2-14.2hh. Mainly black, some bay. Strong, hardy and a full mane and tail. Very sure footed. Temperament said to be friendly, but their strength makes them more suitable for adults.

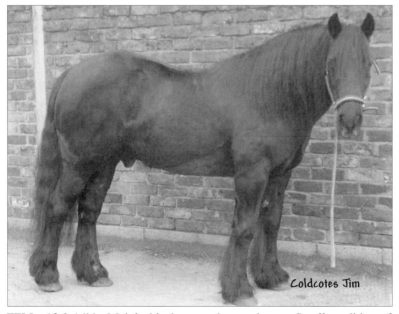

Coldcotes Jim

FELL: 13.2-14hh. Mainly black, some bay and grey. Smaller edition of a Dales, with finer head. Temperament said to be friendly and kind.

WELSH BREEDS

Bronwyn
(Section A Type)

Section A: Up to 12hh. Also known as Welsh Mountain Pony. Usually grey, bay or chestnut, but can be any colour except skewbald/piebald Hardy pony, with a small head. Silky feather. Temperament said to be kind, ideal for children.

Section B: Up to 13.2hh. Taller, finer and more free moving than the A. When shown, the mane and tail may be trimmed. Temperament said to be the same as the A.

Corckhills Charlotte

Section C: Up to 13.2hh. Usually chestnut, bay or black. Cob type sturdy build, with silky feather. Action more extravagant than the A and B, which makes them popular for driving. Temperament said to be more independent than the A and B.

Tynsron Brenin Bach

Section D: Up to 14.2hh, but the ruling may change. Mainly bay, black and chestnut, occasionally grey. Stockiest of the Welsh breeds, with extravagant action, silky fine feather. Excellent to ride or drive. Temperament said to be friendly and strong.

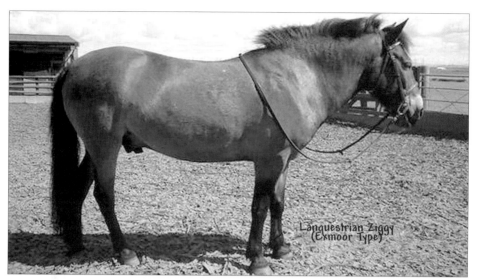

EXMOOR: 12.hh-12.2hh. Bay, with mealy muzzle and area around eyes Very sturdy, with a full mane and tail and a characteristic double coat in the winter. Temperament said to be fairly independent, but good tough ponies.

DARTMOOR: 11.1-12.2hh. Bay, black, grey, occasionally roan and chestnut. Small head. Compact little pony. Temperament said to be kind and gentle.

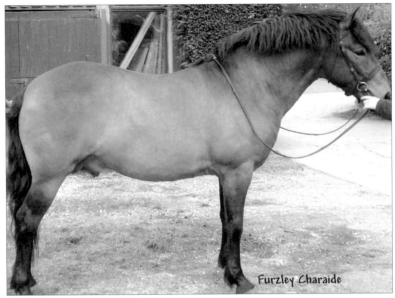

Furzley Charaide

NEW FOREST: 13.2- 14hh. Often bay, but any colour except
skewbald/piebald. The narrowest of the native breeds, making them
very popular and versatile. Temperament said to be friendly.

Carranubber Dolly

CONNEMARA: 14-14.2hh. Mainly grey and dun, some bay and black. The best known
of Irish ponies, popular as competition ponies in all spheres. Temperament said to be
kind and intelligent

Two Totally Different Types of Draught Horses

Whippletree Molly

CLEVELAND BAY has no white except for occasionally a star.15.2-16hh. Slightly convex head. An excellent driving horse and an all rounder for riding. Crossed with a TB they make top class competition horses. Temperament said to be calm and sensible.

SHIRE: Colour bay, black or grey, with white markings on legs. Lots of feather. 16.2-18hh. Can pull heavy loads and are mainly used in agriculture, but can be ridden. Temperament said to be docile and gentle.

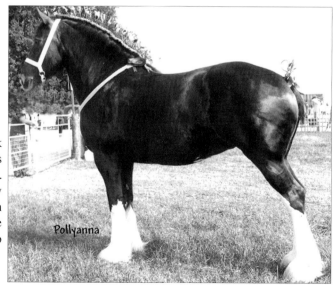

Pollyanna

If they get frightened or excited it can become scary or fascinating, depending on your attitude to the horse! An excited thoroughbred can jump away at any tangent at racing speed, or canter on the spot - not for the faint hearted. However, there are some very calm thoroughbreds, which is why you must include questions about temperament on your checklist.

If your potential purchase has raced, he will need a period of re-training to become used to conventional signals, as he will have been trained with racing as his main task, so can be confused with the change of emphasis in his life. He will also be used to having company all the time and may worry if asked to go out on his own. Riding a well trained thoroughbred can be an addictive pastime, as the quality of the paces can be second to none.

Warmbloods are, as the name implies, a cross between hot bloods, (thoroughbreds) and cold bloods (draught horses).

They are quality non thoroughbreds that are specifically bred, mostly from Continental bloodlines, their name being taken from the area where they are born, e.g: Hanoverian, Oldenburg, Trakkehner,

Warmblood (DHI Star of David)

Dutch and Belgian Warmblood. These horses usually have powerful paces, which are preferable in dressage competitions, and provide the power in jumping, even though they may not have the speed or stamina of the thoroughbred.

The only British Warmblood is probably the Cleveland Bay, which was specifically bred for carriage driving and riding.

The Irish Draught is a very substantial quality horse, and is often crossed with a thoroughbred to produce the **Irish Sports Horse**, renowned for its ability and versatility. A Connemara cross thoroughbred is also a Sports Horse. Irish horses and ponies in general have a good reputation.

Clydesdales and **Shires** are draught horses but can be ridden as well and many are crossed with lighter breeds to produce big powerful horses.

Native ponies, also known as Mountain and Moorland breeds. These are Shetland; Highland; Dales; Fell; Welsh; (There are different sections of Welsh ponies) New Forest; Dartmoor; Exmoor; Connemara. Known for their hardiness and adaptability, but will have varying temperaments and capabilities. The advantage of owning a registered pony is that you can compete in a variety of classes with the same animal. A friend of mine has a Highland, who competes in M & M classes, does M & M working hunter, and her child also takes him in Bonny Pony and "The pony with the nicest tail' classes. He has also taken part successfully in dressage. One factor in caring for native ponies is to appreciate that they are bred to live out most of the time, and can have problems with a rich diet and limited exercise. Most non-pedigree horses will be described by their build.

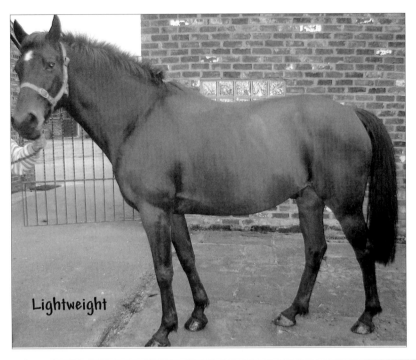

Lightweight

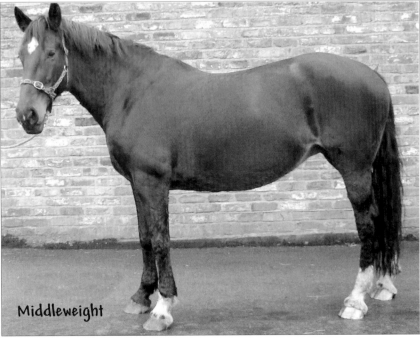

Middleweight

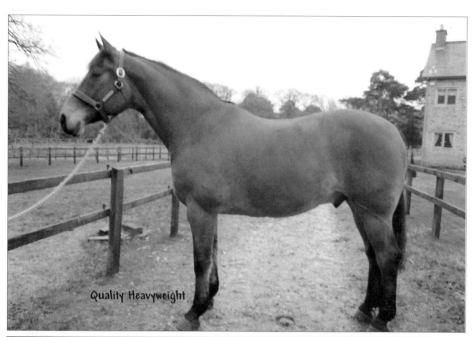

Quality Heavyweight

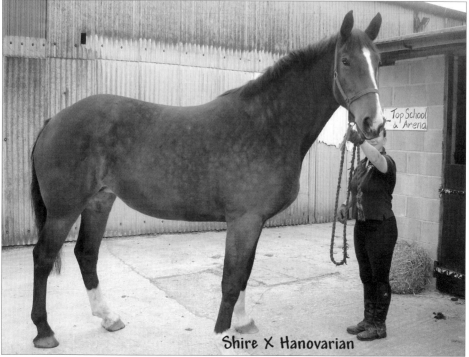

Shire X Hanovarian

Sex

Stallion The handling and care of a stallion or a colt is specialised and cannot be advised for a first time owner.

Geldings are castrated males, and therefore do not normally demonstrate the dominant characteristics of a stallion. As with mares, some are placid, others are lively, most in between.

Mares come into season every three or four weeks during the summer, which may cause problems in a few cases if ridden close to other horses, but this is not common. When mares are in season any geldings in the field may become protective of them. This can be a potential cause of fighting. Some places keep mares and geldings in separate fields, and others leave them in a herd type situation.

Both mares and geldings will vary enormously in their individual temperaments. It is your task to decide which temperament you prefer.

COLOURS

This is a purely personal thing, although white tails will need washing more often! Grey horses often become whiter with age. There an old saying, 'A good horse is never a bad colour'.

Bay Varying shades of brown, with a black mane and tail and points, that is, black from the knee or hock downwards, unless there is a white marking. Can be very dark, or a brighter shade of brown

Dun Beige or khaki colour, with black mane and tail

Piebald Black and white patches. Referred to as coloured.

Skewbald Any other colour with white patches, often brown, but can be tri-coloured.

Grey Varies from nearly white to dark, steel grey, or dappled. Dark coloured ones often lighten with age.

Palomino Golden/cream with a white mane and tail. This is a colour, not a breed as is sometimes thought

Chestnut Various shades of auburn/ ginger, with the same coloured mane and tail Very dark shade is known as liver chestnut. A lighter mane and tail is called flaxen

Appaloosa Generally refers to horses with a spotted coat. Either just on the quarters or all over.

Because there is no equation to find the compatibility of a horse and rider, if you stick with your checklist as a base line, you will soon know if the right horse has come along when you ride him.

Go through your checklist to ensure that your criteria applies ......

TEMPERAMENT

This should really have been at the top of the list.

Choosing a horse with a temperament that you can cope with is so important. Temperament before looks is a good guideline, if he has both, great. (The exception would be with a show horse) The balance between exercise, feeding and stabling can affect the personality and temperament of many horses. It takes experience to recognise if changes in regime are affecting the horse's temperament.

For a family horse, especially with children, a kind tempered friendly horse is needed.

Most owners will want a horse that is easy to catch, tack up, groom, and be safe in the stable. Horses with less than desirable temperaments are often great to ride, but need experienced handlers to avoid conflict. Horses that threaten to kick or bite can be managed in the right home and many excellent horses have quirks that could be daunting to some, such as being difficult to mount, tack up or catch. Some well-known competition horses do not go down the road on their own, and it is on record that many racehorses do not want to be in the lead!

Sparky, totally outgrown by his original owner, but still giving hours of pleasure to other small jockeys.

Training and behaviour

Preferably very well trained, but not always possible. The bottom line is that the horse needs to be accustomed to taking part in whichever sphere you wish to pursue, even in a limited way. If hacking is your main intention, a horse that has always hunted with company, or raced in company, cannot be presumed to hack out alone, although many will. A horse that is competing in dressage or showing may not like jumping. Many jumping horses are not ideal for dressage, and so on.

That is why I stress the importance of having your checklist before you begin looking at horses, so that you will not have to try to change the way a horse goes straight away. When you are familiar with him, it may be possible to persuade him to do all sorts, but try to start off with your basic foundation.

Clyde changing from riding to driving, the whole family involved in the training

131

Now to the exciting and daunting part, finding and viewing!!!

Presuming that you are in contact with other owners at livery yards /riding club or riding schools, it is a good idea to mention that you are looking for a horse. Word of mouth can be one effective way of making contact, with the bonus of knowing the horse's history. Farriers, tack shops and feed merchants often know of horses for sale and will usually know their background. A good factor. Enquire from other owners where they bought from, it may be from a dealer who is used to matching riders and ponies/horses. A reputable dealer will try his best to suit you with a horse, as that is how they stay in business. It is not always possible to trace a horse's past, often you can only guess, although the introduction of passports has made tracking easier. Mind you, a horse that was totally unsuitable for one owner could be just what another person had been searching for!

Many horses are advertised in local or national magazines such as the Horse and Hound and on the Internet. The notice board at saddlers or feed merchants is worth looking at, as it will be easier to check up on a local horse. Enjoy reading these, checking if there are any important omissions, such as easy to catch, good on the road, even the word 'sound'. When a vet has signed a passport, he has signed to say he has seen it, not vetted it as sound.

A client insists that I tell the tale of when he was looking for a gentle horse for himself, a novice, to 'tag along' with his experienced wife, he saw an advert for a horse ridden by a 14 year old girl. Thinking that if the horse was quiet enough for a girl, he should feel safe riding it, he phoned his wife to tell her of the advert. She burst into peals of laughter and said all the 14 year olds she knew loved to gallop, prance and jump big fences, not plod along admiring the view!

There are horse auctions all over the country where the overall prices are usually lower than private sales. As with any auction, buyer beware, as it is totally your knowledge that can determine if the horse would be suitable. It is often a place to sell if the owner cannot sell him privately for a multitude of reasons, some very strange, (such as lying down each time it was tacked up and the rider approached!) but it may be that another person could cope with the situation. Horses can thrive in a different environment. If you do buy from an auction, there may be a vet on site, so have it vetted before you pay for it. Thoroughly read the conditions of sale, which are binding as soon as the hammer drops. There is usually a stipulated time in which to notify any problem, from one hour to 24 hours. These conditions vary at different auctions. If a horse is sold 'as it stands' or unwarranted, on your head be it. You may have the bargain of the month, or a heap of trouble. You will not be able to try the horse in different situations, so I cannot recommend this way to obtain your first horse, although there are bargains to be had.

After you have studied a few adverts or have a list through word of mouth, take a pause and go through your checklist to ensure that your criteria applies. When you phone to arrange a viewing, it is best to write a query list to have at your side. Include such things as:

- Check the description in the advert, and ask about the age
- Has the horse got a passport?
- Why is it being sold?
- How long have you owned him?
- Where did he come from?
- Describe his temperament (before you say which temperament you prefer)
- How does he behave in traffic on his own and with others?
- Is he easy to catch and how is his behaviour with other horses?
- What is the perceived level of training? (this can vary enormously, depending

on the ability of the rider)

- Is he in regular work, if not, why and when last ridden?
- Has he competed, if so when was he last out at a competition and was he placed?
- Is he easy to load and travel?
- Have there been any injuries recently?
- Does he live mainly stabled or out in the field?
- Has he ever had laminitis or sweet itch?
- Is he shod, and good with farrier?
- Has he been clipped and was he relatively calm?
- Is the horse open to vetting? If the answer no, leave it alone.
- Check that the person who is selling the horse is the owner.
- Who has ridden the horse mostly? If a strong, experienced man is the main rider, the horse may react differently to a lightweight lady.

This list is long, but all these facts need establishing to try to find the best horse for you. Tell the advertiser/seller what you are proposing to do with the horse and ask if they think it will be suitable for you.

Arrange to go early in the day to view the horse so you get a feel of how he normally responds. If two or three potential buyers had already ridden him, he may be tired or worried when you rode him.

You will need experienced moral support to accompany you, a person who knows your ability and lifestyle. If the sellers state that they do not like advisors with you, leave it. The majority of horses are on the market for genuine reasons, but do take an experienced companion with you to be a witness to how the horse behaves and is described. Expect to be questioned about where and how will you keep him, as the owner should have the horse's welfare at heart, and want re-assurance that he is going to a knowledgeable home.

Determine if the price is negotiable, sometimes it can be to the appropriate home, and is the tack included? Remember that if you are answering an advert, your time to decide is limited, so be as thorough as possible when you are viewing. It is a big decision that you are taking, as the horse will be a big part of your life from the moment he arrives.

If you are viewing a horse belonging to a dealer there will probably be time to try him out more than once, but quite a few of the questions on your check list won't be answered as the horse may not have been there long enough. Horse dealers earn their living by matching riders and horses together, and so even though all the questions cannot be answered, they will have a good idea of suitability of you and the horse. They will want you to be a satisfied customer and recommend them to others. It is known that some potential owners ask a dealer to look out for a horse for them, and are prepared to wait till a suitable one is found.

Go and look at suitable sounding horses with an open mind, as some advertisers do get carried away when describing the virtues of their horse and can be blind to the horse's faults. One person's idea of a '*good jumper*' could mean clearing two feet high, whilst another could mean four feet. '*Ridden by children*' could mean that they were always led! In other words, the pony is not safe off the lead rein. Or the children have been riding awkward ponies since they were five, and the whole family are experienced horse riders/trainers!

I have looked at adverts recently and the 'in' word at present seems to be 'stunning'. We recently went to see a stunning horse that was advertised, who dished and cantered around sideways with his head in the air, the smiling owner still maintaining how stunning he was!

He dished and cantered around sideways with his head in the air ....

Have a good look at him before he is tacked up, and see him standing in the yard, noting his behaviour. Watch him trotted up, especially to see if he dishes, which is not the end of the world, but could have repercussions for strenuous competitions.

See the horse ridden for a few minutes, and ask to see him perform what you need your horse to do. Pay particular attention to watching if there is any tendency to 'nap' towards the stables or any other horses, as this would signify a problem from the start.

If it is obvious that he is not the one for you, simply say that he is not what you want and nobody will have wasted his or her time.

Gina trying out a young horse over small fences, as she wants a horse to compete in one day events. As he already works on his own, he seems to have the ability to be a good horse for this rider.

If you like what you see then ride him yourself to get the feel of the stride, obedience, size. **DO** remember to try what your main interests are, for example small jumps, ride in a field, ride on the road, alone if need be, checking first with the owner that they are sure the horse will be all right with you on board doing these things. If dressage or schooling is your main aim, the horse must be reasonably supple and obedient so that you can progress. Please do not buy a horse just because it has a nice face or you feel sorry for him!

If you get good vibes from the horse, arrange to go back and ride him again. If you are planning to travel the horse regularly, ask to see him being loaded.

This time catch and tack up without assistance. Pick out his feet and generally handle the horse to make sure you will feel confident on your own with him.

Ask the owner to provide a written warranty stating that the horse is as described in the advert and has no vices such as crib biting or weaving, and how long the warranty is for, probably a week. Once more read through your checklist, and if all seems to be ok, you can begin to get excited! Ask to see his passport just to check it meets the description, and the horse is owned by the person who is selling it.

You should look at quite a few horses before you decide, but once you have definitely decided to go ahead with having your own, do this over a short period as the good ones will not be on the market for long.

The perfect pony, calm at home with seven year old rider, and capable at showing in hand with big sister.

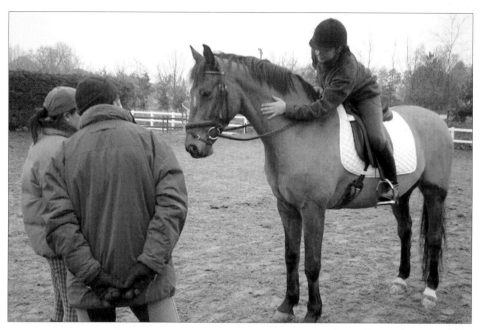

You will need experienced moral support to accompany you.

If you are planning to travel the horse regularly, ask to see him being loaded.

When the right horse is found you could broach the option of having the horse on trial, but many people are against this. Horses are at their most vulnerable when they change homes and surroundings and can damage themselves. You could offer to insure the horse first, but if a trial is not forthcoming, handle and ride the horse in all situations that you may come across.

When you have agreed on price, arrange to have the horse vetted as described earlier. It is worth writing out an agreement stating that you will have the horse subject to a satisfactory vetting and will then collect it and take possession on a certain day. Occasionally a horse has damaged itself between vetting and delivery, and the prospective new owner does not want to take delivery, even though it is not the seller's fault.

Vets can pick up problems that even the owner may not have known, such as a heart or lung problem, eye problem or faults in confirmation. Small sarcoids can go unnoticed to the owner, but can be serious if not controlled. Even non-suspected lameness can show up if the horse is ridden or lunged on circles. The vet will discuss his findings with you. If everything is ok ....

**HORSE OWNING DAY
WILL HAVE ARRIVED!**

***** GOOD LUCK TO
BOTH OF YOU *****

10
THE FIRST FEW WEEKS

"What a sharp learning curve" - Jeanette, DIY first timer
"Total disruption, loving every minute" - The Jackson family's first pony
"Just as stressful as fetching a new baby home" - Sheila, first time owner after her children had left home

Have an in depth conversation with the person in charge of your new horse before you change his home. Establish exactly what he has to eat daily and at what times he is fed. If he is mostly stabled and turned out for a while each day, find out for how long. You will need to know how much, in weight, hay he has daily.

With a horse living out there will still be a routine, as you presume that he is handled each day. Again find out if he has a concentrate feed daily and if so, how much, or is he just on grass?

His current exercise routine needs to be noted and try to stay near the same timing at first. It is important to know how experienced the previous rider was and to be aware that a change of rider can change some horses dramatically.

Before the horse is collected, have insurance cover in place, as you are the owner as soon as the money changes hands.

Taking delivery of your first horse is very exciting as well as daunting. You will need to have already arranged tack fitting if his previous tack had not come with him. If he is living out, the field will have needed checking for any weak places, and other owners informed that a new horse will be joining the group. It will still be best to have your new horse stabled for a day or two, so that you can keep an eye on him.

Stables need checking to remove anything that the horse can catch himself on if he is whirling around, as some do in a new environment.

The farrier you are going to use should be already booked in, as they all need a few weeks' notice. Your favourite riding instructor could be told, if she did not already know, so that you could call her (or him) for any reason if you felt the need. Arrange to spend as much time as possible around the horse for the first few days, not necessarily riding, but handling morning and evening at least, to begin the building up of trust and companionship between you both.

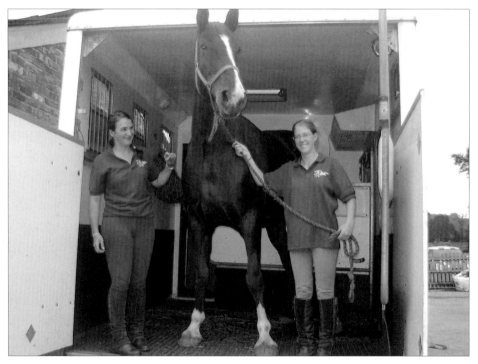

Have the horse delivered in daylight, so that he can look around. It will help if you can have fetched some of the hard feed and hay that he had been eating, so that it can be mixed gradually with the feed you are using. A sudden change of food could

make him ill, so if this is not possible stay to mainly hay or grass to begin with and only introduce the different food gradually, over at least ten days. Try to stay around as much as possible to start with, so that he associates you with reassurance.

Do not be alarmed if he prances around as he is unloaded, it is fairly normal behaviour (for a few minutes). Expect the horse to whinny and be unsettled at first, maybe running around the box, as he has left his companions and not yet found any more. Grooming is a good way to bond with your new horse and will help him to settle.

The first time you ride him, preferably the next day, keep the task simple, you both will have to find out the different responses to your aids, which may be different than the previous rider. Be prepared to have company initially till the horse is relaxed in his new surroundings. Horses naturally tend to be a bit excited in new surroundings, so expect some whinnying and staring at new objects at first, but this should soon wear off. Remember to always have a headcollar on the horse at all times when you are handling, grooming etc, as a horse walking around as you are trying to brush, tack up, is not treating you as being in charge!

Stick to the same amount of work and feed and turnout as his previous home to start with, and only change this after your assessment of how you wish him to alter. Remember that the horse will be in a totally new environment and will know nothing about your routine or habits. You will probably know nothing about his previous encounters with lots of situations and it becomes quite a steep learning curve for you both. As the horse cannot tell us if anything is worrying him, occasionally step back and look at a situation from the horse's perception, although I do not advocate assuming that the horse has the same reasoning powers that we have.

Good trainers have the knack of interpreting horse/rider combinations in different situations, so if problems arise that would be a good first port of call. In the event of problems arising, get in touch with the sellers straight away, as they should be able to help you. This is why it is best to have had a companion when you view, as witness to what was said at the time. A contract or warranty at time of sale will have helped to clarify the situation.

Introduce him gradually to the other horses, each place will have a system they use to do this. Groups of horses always have a pecking order, which causes some fighting if a new member is suddenly introduced. Once the order is settled, large numbers can live peacefully together. The boss horse is often a mare.

Make a record card with all his details, including his temperature and pulse at rest as well as the vaccinations due, shoeing, vet phone number, your address etc.

Over the first few weeks you will find that the horse begins to recognise your voice and footsteps, and even the sound of your car. Even if the horse is at livery and somebody else feeds him, the time spent grooming, handling and riding will soon help the horse to realise you are special. It is a great feeling to be greeted by your horse, as it shows that he has accepted you as his new owner. He will probably start to come to you when you go to the field, though this is not guaranteed.

You will gradually find out his likes and dislikes, his reactions in differing situations, if he is generally laid back or active, and any little foibles that he has, there can be many! My horse can't stand cotton thread tickling on his forehead, so it has to be a very quick plait undoing, making sure the thread is removed instantly.

The first time this happened I thought he was having a fit, but it was just his little foible.

You will soon get to notice what is his normal behaviour, such as if he mixes with the other horses in the field, or if he is a loner, or even if he has a favourite friend. In the stable he may be tidy or messy, and eat his food quickly or take his time, both are normal. The reason you need to know his normal behaviour is that any changes from this can be indicators that all is not well and you will need to keep an eye on him.

A new first time owner, Joanna, was quite happy to let me take an extract from a letter she wrote to me shortly after buying her horse. She had been helping at the stables for about six months before actually getting the horse, and had known him for that time as being friendly and uncomplicated.

"….the first ten days he was as well behaved as when I was trying him out, but then turned into a hooligan. I could not catch him, and then he kept pulling me where he wanted to go and would not come with me. When I rode him I could not make him go and I also had trouble picking out his feet, he just kept stamping them down each time I picked them up. In desperation I asked the girls on the yard for help, and they showed me how to be very positive with my actions with him. I had been so nervous and not wanting to upset him in any way, he had not accepted me as his leader. With their help, he soon returned to his normal happy self and is now the best horse in the world"

By taking time and thought before owning a horse, and planning for what you are expecting to do, you have given yourself an excellent chance of finding your perfect horse. There is a lot written about what to do when you have acquired him, so I hope this book has helped the decision making and that you....

Like owning a horse!

More "Horsey" expressions

Boxy foot   Feet that are more upright than the generally accepted correct angle to the ground.

Breaking   A term given to the initial training of the horse.

Brushing   When the horse knocks the inside of a fetlock with the inside of the other foot, hence needing brushing boots. Often a conformational fault.

Bute   A common name for an inflammatory medication, that is also an analgesic.

Clench   The point of the nail driven into the foot by the farrier, which is then hammered down, to hold the shoe onto the foot.

Cast   When a horse has rolled and is too near a wall to be able to push himself up again, with his legs jammed .

Cut   Another term used for gelding, castration.

Clipping   When the hair is removed so that when a horse sweats, his skin can dry off quickly, which would not happen if the horse had a full winter coat.

Dishing   A way of moving where the lower forelegs move outwards as well as forwards, Unsightly but not often a cause of lameness.

Drag hunting   When the hounds follow a scent.

Ewe neck   Where the horses' neck has very little muscle on his crest and dips in front of the withers.

Feather   The term given to lots of hair around the fetlock area..

Forging   When the toe of the front foot is struck by the toe of the hind foot as the horse trots. It is a sign of an unbalanced horse.

Grass ring	Ridges on the horses hoof, indicating a sudden change of diet or stressful situation.
Hackamore	Bitless bridle.
Hand	Measurement of horses, 4 inches (11cms).
Hippophile	Lover of horses.
Horse sick	Fields that have been overgrazed, and the grass is either long unpalatable patches or bare. Often lots of weeds as well.
In hand	When the horse is led.
Kimblewick	A type of curb bit.
Lateral	When the horse moves forwards and sideways.
List	A dark stripe along the horses back.
Lockjaw	Another name for tetanus.
Martingale	A piece of tack used to prevent the horse getting his head above the angle of control.
Midden	Another word for the muck heap.
Napping	Term to describe a situation when the horse will not go forwards.
Near side	Left hand side.
Off Side	Right side.
Periople	Layer on the outside of the wall of hoof, that keeps the wall moist.
Pulse	In a healthy horse, 36-40 per minute at rest.
Quittor	An abscess that forms on the coronary band, caused by an infection in the foot.
Ragwort	A plant that can cause liver damage to horses if eaten in large enough quantities. Not eaten whilst growing, but if withered or in hay it can be fatal. Good husbandry will include pulling up all ragwort when it appears and burning it.

Respiration rate In a healthy horse, 8-12 per minute. With exercise rises rapidly, and a sign of the horses fitness is how soon his respiration rate settles after exercise.

Spavin A bony enlargement on a hock joint, causing problems in the joint.

Sandcrack A split in the wall of the hoof, causing a weakness. Needs very regular farrier attention to rectify.

Sprain Any degree of tearing of tendon or muscle fibres. All work expected of a horse has to follow a period of exercising to build up strength in tendons and muscles. This is so they can carry out the task without the muscle/ tendon becoming tired.

Stale To urinate.

Stringhalt This is an involuntary snatching up of a hind leg whilst moving. The horse does not appear to feel pain with this and can usually be ridden.

Teeth 36 in mares, with two or four tushes in male horses.

Thoroughpin A soft swelling on the hock joint, unsightly but not normally a cause of lameness.

Urticaria An allergic reaction, causing soft lumps on the body, in varying degrees.

Unlevel Lame.

Vice Regular unpleasant behaviour such as rearing, weaving, crib biting, biting and kicking.

Windgall A swelling of the tendon sheath surrounding the fetlock joint. Not always a cause of lameness, but a sign of wear and tear.

Yew poisoning Fatal.

COLOURS

Bay Varying shades of brown, with a black mane and tail and points, that is, black from the knee or hock downwards, unless there is a white marking. Can be very dark, or a brighter shade of brown.

Dun Beige or khaki colour, with black mane and tail.

Piebald Black and white patches. Referred to as coloured.

Skewbald Any other colour and white patches, often brown, but can be tri coloured.

Grey Varies from nearly white to dark, steel grey, or dappled. Dark coloured ones often lighten with age.

Palomino Golden/cream with a white mane and tail. This is a colour, not a breed as is sometimes thought.

Chestnut Various shades of ginger, with the same coloured mane and tail Very dark shade is known as liver chestnut. A lighter mane and tail is called flaxen.

Appaloosa Generally refers to horses with a spotted coat. Either just on the quarters (blanket spotted) or all over (leopard spotted).

MARKINGS

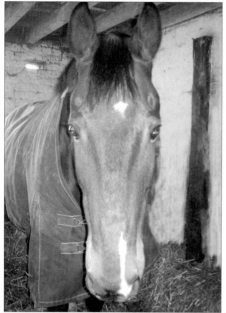

Star: A white marking on the forehead

Snip: A white marking on the muzzle

Sock: A white marking on the leg,
which can be just a very short mark, or
extending from the foot to below the
knee, or hock.
Stocking: A white marking from foot to
above the knee or hock.

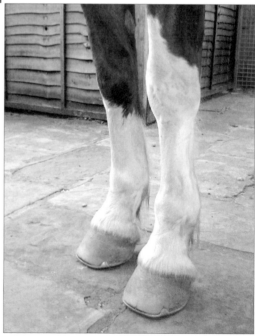

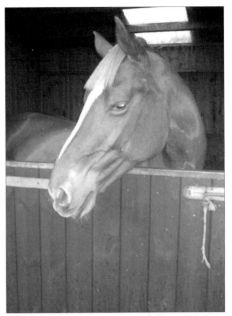

Blaze: A wide white marking, covering the bones on the face.

Stripe: A narrow white marking down the front of the face.

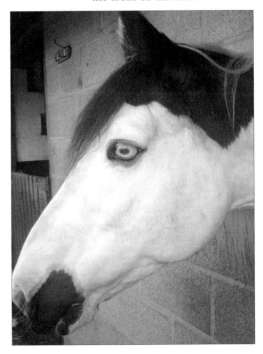

Wall eye: Caused by lack of pigmentation. This condition does not affect the eyesight.

Other options than buying your own

Loaning

This can be mutually beneficial, giving the loaner a chance to decide if they really do have the time to benefit from owning, and the owner a period of not having the necessary commitment.

The owner must be vigilant in checking the credentials of a loaner who is not known to them and pay a visit to where the horse will be kept. It has been known for advertisers to ask for companion horses and then sell them on at a later date. Arrange regular visits to check on the horses welfare. There needs to be a specified time for either party to claim back or return the horse.

This is an agreement between you and the loaner to provide and care for a horse in a specified way and time. Must be on a legally binding contract, which needs to specify who pays for;

Livery

Insurance

Maintenance of tack/equipment

Shoeing

Worming

First Aid/Vet

Arrange regular visits to
check on the horses welfare.

The British Horse Society can provide a copy of a loan agreement, which will help you to be thorough in your checking. It also gives a guideline for the wording of the agreement.

Points to clarify

- Any restrictions on rider or use.
- Notice needed if the loan ceases.
- Situations when the owner will take the horse back and who pays for disposal if he dies.

DONKEYS

All the guidance about time and commitment also applies to the donkey, but for differences in the care and husbandry please refer to the Donkey Breed Society, as the needs of donkeys do differ from those of horses.

Sponsorship

Not really owning a horse, but having an involvement that can be extremely satisfying. The sponsorship can cover any disciplines and is a personal arrangement between the rider and sponsor. This can be discreet, or the rider wears sponsorship clothing, and he will be in a Public Relations position whilst at events. The horsebox and equipment may also have the logo/name displayed.

Many important events make concessions for owners, and will have hospitality arrangements for them.

Many partnerships are very successful, with the owner having the satisfaction of watching their horse compete in good hands. Obviously there has to be commitment on both sides, with both owner and rider agreeing terms. Very often the sponsor will pay the training fees for a specified period of time. The sponsor really needs to be quite experienced in equine matters to appreciate the time necessary for training, and also the probability of the horse being side lined for various reasons.

Syndicate

Being part of a syndicate means that a few people share the costs of the horse and its training costs between them. There are many syndicates especially in the racing world, but in any discipline, especially when the horse is very valuable. If you are interested in becoming part of a syndicate, find some friends who do not necessarily need to make a profit from owning part of a horse, and attend events that interest you. Some syndicates are advertised but many are by word of mouth. As there are only a few people in a racing syndicate, it is more personal than an owners club.

One of my friends is in a racing syndicate, and when their horses finish racing, he has them at his farm. He learned to ride, and now has four ex-racehorses!

Racing Club

Joining a racing club can give a sense of involvement and be another way to make like-minded friends. You will pay an annual fee, and some arrangements give you a share of any profits, but don't bank on it. It can give a real interest to the races that the horse is in, and be quite nerve racking as an owner watching the racing.

A large racing club will provide regular newsletters to the members, keeping them up to date with the progress of their horses. If the club breeds its own horses, it adds another interest for the members, who can follow the horses' progress from birth to racing. All clubs arrange visits to the trainer's yards and often members watch the horses whilst they are training on the gallops.

Fostering

Caring for a horse that belongs to a welfare organisation. This entails approaching the association, which is usually a charity, to offer a home to one of their horses/ponies. Some of their charges are fit and able, and are offered to suitable homes on a loan basis.

Most of these horses will have had a difficult patch in their life, so you need to be very aware of this. Some will be schooled for riding or driving, but many will be as companions only.

Prospective loaners will be invited to the centre to be assessed and matched with a suitable horse. Following several visits, and assuming that both horse and carer are judged to be compatible the fostering arrangement can proceed.

Your facilities will be rigorously checked, with regular inspections of the horse. If caring for a horse, not riding, is your main interests, you would still be welcome to have a pony/horse that could not be ridden for a variety of reasons.

One of these reasons may come as a great and unexpected surprise, and you may find that you get a little more than you bargained for!

So you'd like to own a horse?

USEFUL ADDRESSES

Association of British Riding Schools
Queen's Chambers, 38-40 Queen Street, Penzance, Cornwall TR18 4BH

British Horse Society
Stoneleigh Deer Park, Kenilworth, Warwickshire, CV8 2XZ

British Riding Club
Stoneleigh Deer Park, Kenilworth, Warwickshire, CV8 2XZ

Pony Club
Stoneleigh Park, Kenilworth, Warwickshire, CV8 2RW

List of Veterinary Practitioners
Royal College of Veterinary Surgeons, 7 Mansfield Street, London, W1G 9NQ

List of Farriers

Farrier's Registration Council, Sefton House, Adam Court, Newark Road

Peterborough RE1 5PP

Donkey Breed Society

secretary@donkeybreedsociety.co.uk

National Equine Welfare Council

10 Wales Street, King's Sutton, Banbury,

Oxon OX17 3RR

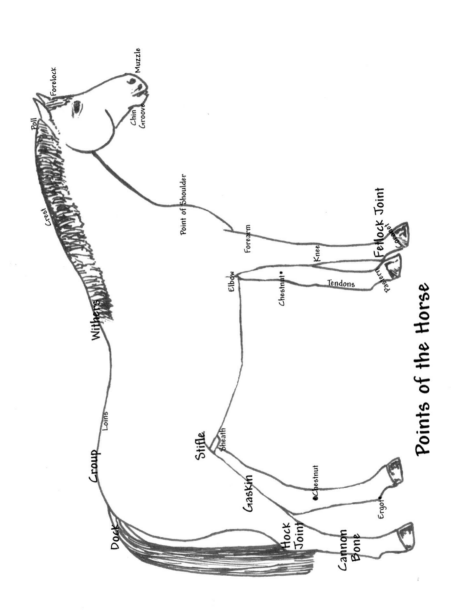

Points of the Horse

Acknowledgments

The top of the list in these Acknowledgments has to go to the late Albert Booth, from whom I learnt so much about horses.

Also the staff and clients at Mobberley Riding School for their help and support. So many people have been generous with their time and encouragement during the process of turning my ideas into the reality of this book, and I would like to use this as an opportunity to say thank you to them all - they know who they are!
Many others, too numerous to mention individually, have shared advice, anecdotes and the loan of their photographs, which have greatly enriched this book.

My thanks must go to Christine Pemberton, who has patiently guided me through the process of converting my sheaves of paper into a coherent book, and to Lisa Gort and Richard Creasey for their cartoons.

Finally of course, to all the horses that I have ever known, each with his own individual personality.